Preparing to work
in
adult social
care

Caul...on

LEVEL 3

Clare Cape
Mark Walsh
Pat Ayling
Janet McAleavy

Nelson Thornes

Published in 2012 by:
Nelson Thornes Ltd
Delta Place
27 Bath Road
CHELTENHAM
GL53 7TH
United Kingdom

12 13 14 15 16 / 10 9 8 7 6 5 4 3 2 1

A catalogue record for this book is available from the British Library

ISBN 978 1 4085 1813 7

Cover photograph: Douglas Forbes
Illustrations by Katherine Baxendale and Angela Knowles
Page make-up by GreenGate Publishing Services, Tonbridge, Kent
Printed and bound in Spain by Graphycems

Acknowledgements

ppiv, v Reed Social Care; p1 Fred Froese/iStockphoto; p2 Yuri Arcurs/Fotolia; p4 MarkCoffeyPhoto/iStockphoto; p5 Monkey Business/Fotolia; p9 Alexander Raths/Fotolia; p10 delihayat/iStockphoto; p12 auremar/Fotolia; p19 WoodyStock/Alamy; p24 Rich Legg/iStockphoto; p27 detailblick/Fotolia; p31 Paul Doyle/Alamy; p34 Odua Images/Fotolia; p36 fstop123/iStockphoto; p40 pixdeluxe/iStockphoto; p42 Monkey Business/Fotolia; p45 Ocskay Bence/Fotolia; p46 webphotographeer/iStockphoto; p61 Rob/Fotolia; p79 John Birdsall/Photofusion Picture Library; p85 Paula Solloway/Alamy; p87 Ulrike Preuss/Photofusion Picture Library; p91 VikramRaghuvanshi/iStockphoto; p95 M Itani/Alamy; p96 Christa Stadtler/Photofusion Picture Library; p99 technotr/iStockphoto; p105 Chris Schmidt/iStockphoto; p114 CEFutcher/iStockphoto; p127 tiero/Fotolia; p130 Deklofenak/Fotolia; p132 p138 nano/iStockphoto; p140 skegbydave/iStockphoto; p132 Alina555/iStockphoto; p166 kali9/iStockphoto; p176 Franck Boston/Fotolia; p177 pressmaster/Fotolia; p179 Fancy/Alamy; p181 Toshiro Shimada/Getty; p189 Visage/Getty.

Reed Social Care would like to acknowledge the following contributors: Circle, Coventry City Council, Places for People.

We would also like to acknowledge the following contributors from within Reed Social Care:
Niall Morgan, Leslie Weare, Gladys Wright, Helen Clark, Jason Paterson, Rav Grewal, Catherine Maskell, Chris Quy.

Gladwell, M, *Blink: The Power of Thinking Without Thinking*, Penguin, 2006.

Coulter, A, *Implementing shared decision making in the UK*, The Health Foundation, 2010. www.health.org.uk/publications/implementing-shared-decision-making-in-the-uk/

The copyright and all other intellectual property rights in the material to be reproduced are owned by, or licensed to, the Commission for Equality and Human Rights, known as the Equality and Human Rights Commission ('the EHRC').

Contents

Introduction

Reed Social Care and Community Care

Reed Social Care is the UK's leading recruitment consultancy for high-quality, dedicated social care staff. From a nationwide network of offices, we find work for qualified and unqualified social workers, community support and residential work professionals, throughout the public and private sectors. For those people who come to work for Reed, we offer industry-leading training and support, to allow people to progress their careers.

Reed Community Care provides support and carers directly to those in the community. We run extensive training courses, and offer support throughout, in order to provide the best possible care to the people we work with.

Entering the adult social care job market

The social care job market is a challenging one to enter at the present time, particularly in the public sector where budget cuts mean that organisations are seeking to employ only the highest-quality staff that they can find. Managers are looking for professional, conscientious employees who really want to work in the social care sector, and who display commitment and enthusiasm for supporting the people that they care for on a daily basis.

However, an ageing population also means increased demand for high-quality care staff – something that will only continue for the foreseeable future, as a greater proportion of the population requires support and care. With the right help and application, you really could find yourself in a job for life.

The purpose of this book is to help you to complete your Level 3 Preparing to Work in Adult Social Care qualification and to gain your certificate. It also aims to help give you the tools to get a job in the adult social care sector, through work based examples and Reed employment hints and tips.

Expert help

As the leading recruitment consultancy for social care staff in the UK, Reed Social Care is ideally placed to advise new workers on entering the sector, from building a CV, to finding work experience and interviewing for the ideal job for you. We help hundreds of people each week to find work, in both temporary and permanent positions, and we want to share our experience with you.

That's why, throughout this book, you will find helpful hints from our highly experienced consultants, all designed towards helping you find that perfect job in adult social care. These tips range from advice on CV writing, to interview tips and techniques, all linked in with the learning material in the book.

As well as this, Reed Social Care has gained insights from some of our biggest clients – leading recruiters within the adult social care sector, to help you understand the mindset of a potential employer. This includes the traits and skills that they would like to see in their new employees, why you need the skills taught in this book, and how they are used on a day-to-day basis within their organisations.

This is invaluable information and offers unique insight, all geared towards helping you gain a position within adult social care.

reed.co.uk

Throughout the book, there will also be regular mention of reed.co.uk.

reed.co.uk is the UK's number 1 jobsite, featuring jobs advertised by many different employers, as well as posts advertised by Reed's consultants on behalf of their clients.

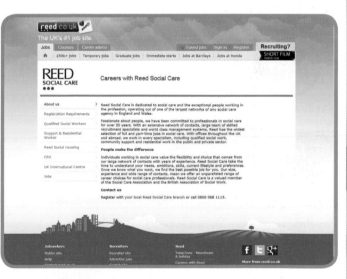

All of the positions advertised on the site are listed by sector, and are easily searchable by location, salary and type of position, to make finding a position which is right for you as easy as possible.

reed.co.uk allows you to register as an individual user and to create and download your CV online, using advice from the experts along the way. There will be regular advice throughout this book to help you to improve your CV and covering letter, and use it to apply for the positions which are right for you.

reed.co.uk is an ideal starting point for those looking to find a job within adult social care, and provides all the tools to allow you to improve your career prospects while learning with this book.

About this book

Welcome to your Preparing to Work in Adult Social Care Level 3 Course Book. The purpose of this book is to help you complete your Level 3 Preparing to Work in Adult Social Care Certificate. This book gives complete coverage of the qualification and includes expert employment advice from Reed Social Care to help you get a job.

This colourful text is packed full of activities to check what you have learnt and there are also exclusive tips from Reed Social Care.

The book's features include:

Unit opener – this page contains a brief introduction to each unit along with the learning outcomes you need to achieve.

'Think about', which encourage you to think about issues in health and social care

'Find out!', which encourage you to do further research

'Did you know?', with key supporting information, such as legislation you should be aware of

Reed social care @work give insights from employers into which skills they value in their staff

Key Terms

'Key terms' – during your course you'll come across new words that you may not have heard before. These words are in bold in the text and the definitions have been provided.

In Practice
What would you do?

'In Practice' and 'What would you do?' – a range of real life examples of different scenarios to provide context to the topics covered. Some of them ask how you would approach the problem.

Reed social care tips are designed to help you get a job.

Your questions answered

'Your questions answered' – your expert authors answer some burning questions you may have as you work through the units.

'Quick Quiz' – at the end of each unit you will find ten multiple choice questions which recap what you should have learnt in the unit. Check your answers to the Quick Quiz questions with your tutor. Answers can also be found in the 'Care' section of www.planetvocational.co.uk.

Good luck!

Principles of **safeguarding and** protection in **health and social care**

This unit introduces the important area of safeguarding and protecting individuals from abuse. It identifies different types of abuse, and the signs which could indicate that abuse is occurring. It also considers when individuals might be vulnerable to abuse and what you should do if you suspect abuse. A range of factors contributes to the vulnerability of individuals who use social care services. There are some important national policies and local systems in place to protect and safeguard them. This unit focuses on the social care worker's role in this process, as well as the roles of other professionals and agencies.

On completion of this unit you should:

- know how to recognise signs of abuse
- know how to respond to suspected or alleged abuse
- understand the national and local context of safeguarding and protection from abuse
- understand ways to reduce the likelihood of abuse
- know how to recognise and report unsafe practices

4.1 Recognising signs of abuse

Abuse can take many forms

What is 'abuse'?

Most adults can protect themselves from threats of harm – they are not **vulnerable** to abuse. However, some adults who use social care services may need **safeguarding** because they are at greater risk of, or have already experienced, abuse.

In 2000 the Department of Health published *No Secrets* which defined abuse as: 'a violation of an individual's human and civil rights by any other person or persons'.

Abuse can occur when individuals are deprived of their rights to:

- privacy
- independence
- choose for themselves
- a decent quality of life
- protection and security.

Adults in need of safeguarding can experience different types of abuse and sometimes more than one type of abuse. For example, emotionally abusive threats and intimidation often happen at the same time as physical abuse or violence. Protecting **adults at risk** of abuse is a key responsibility of every social care worker.

Vulnerable More likely to suffer risk and harm.

Safeguarding Ensuring the individual is safe from abuse and neglect, and helping people to make choices independently.

Adult at risk Anyone aged 18 years and over who might not be able to protect themselves because they are ill, disabled or older.

Key Terms

did you know?

In 2010–2011, older people reported the most incidences of abuse (61 per cent), followed by adults with a physical disability (49 per cent), clients with mental health problems (23 per cent), learning disabled clients (20 per cent) and adults experiencing substance misuse or other problems (7 per cent).

Type of abuse	Definition of abuse
Physical	Deliberate use of force that results in bodily injury or pain. Includes hitting, biting, shaking, burning, inappropriate treatments, isolation or confinement and misuse of medication.
Sexual	Involvement in sexual activity without consent. This may be direct (e.g. being forced to perform sex acts) or indirect (being forced to watch sexual activity in person or on the TV or internet). The person may not wish to **consent**, lack **capacity**, or they may feel **coerced** because the abuser is in a position of trust, power or authority.
Emotional/ psychological	Any action that damages an individual's mental well-being such as threats, humiliation, bullying, swearing or other mental cruelty that results in distress. Includes the denial of basic human rights, such as choice, self-expression, privacy and dignity.
Financial	The theft or misuse of an individual's money or personal possessions.
Institutional	Mistreatment of an individual by the authorities or people within an institution. It occurs when the routines, systems and **norms** of an institution are seen as more important than the needs of the people they support.
Self-neglect	When an individual fails to care for themselves and meet their own basic needs for food, warmth, rest, medical care and personal care. May be intentional (such as self-harm) or unintentional, due to physical or mental health issues.
Neglect by others	Failure to meet an individual's needs for personal care, food, warmth, rest, medical care, social stimulation, cultural or religious needs. This can be either acts of **omission** (not doing something) or **commission** (doing something on purpose).

Types and examples of abuse

Consent Giving informed agreement to or permission for something to happen, such as an action or decision. Establishing consent varies according to individual's assessed capacity to give consent.

Capacity The mental or physical ability to do something.

Coerce Force someone to do something against their will.

Norm Accepted, normal behaviour.

Omission Where something is either deliberately or accidentally not done.

Commission Deliberately doing something while knowing the consequences.

Key Terms

Indicators of physical abuse

Physical abuse is the easiest to recognise – you can usually see the results of it. However, it can be missed if someone makes excuses for it and some forms of physical abuse – such as denying an individual's needs or the misuse of medication – can also be more difficult to spot. If an explanation doesn't 'fit' an injury, you should always report it and ask for further investigation.

Some signs of physical abuse can be easy to spot

Signs and symptoms of physical abuse include:

- multiple or minor bruising of different areas with inconsistent explanations

- burns and scalds, including oddly shaped bruising or burns – such as the shape of an iron, weapon or cigarette end

- marks on the skin from being slapped, scratched, bitten or pinched

- broken bones or unexplained falls

- evidence of old injuries, for example untreated broken bones

- indicators of malnutrition or general signs of neglect

- misuse of medication, such as not giving pain relief or giving too much sedative

- defensive reactions by the individual when approached by anyone.

Indicators of sexual abuse

Sexual abuse can include contact or non-contact abuse:

- 'Contact' sexual abuse includes: vaginal or anal rape; touching someone or forcing someone to touch another person in a sexual way without consent.

- 'Non-contact' sexual abuse includes: indecent exposure; sexual talk, harassment or inappropriate photography; forcing a person to watch pornography or sexual activity.

Sexual abuse is often associated with the misuse of power, alongside physical and psychological abuse.

Signs and symptoms of sexual abuse include:

- fear of physical contact
- injury, bleeding, irritation or infection around the genitals
- sexually transmitted disease
- bruising, bites, scratches on the breast or inner thigh
- inappropriate conversations of a sexual nature
- unexplained crying and distress
- withdrawal from social contact
- self-harm or self-neglect.

Indicators of emotional or psychological abuse

Psychological abuse can be difficult to identify, as it is usually hidden. Sometimes those committing this kind of abuse withhold care, friendship and love, make verbal threats to frighten the individual into doing what they want, or deny them the right to make decisions.

Signs and symptoms of emotional and psychological abuse include:

- self-isolation – especially if the person was previously friendly with others
- sadness, depression or uncontrollable crying
- being passive with no spontaneous smiles or laughter
- fear or anxiety, especially about being alone or with particular people
- increased tension or irritability or attention-seeking behaviour
- low self-esteem and lack of self-confidence
- changes in appetite and sleep patterns, for example nightmares or insomnia
- self-abuse or self-harm, for example misuse of alcohol, nicotine or illegal drugs, refusing food or medication.

Isolation is a type of abuse

Bill Eastham, aged 92, is a resident in The Brook residential and nursing home. Bill was a prisoner of war for most of the Second World War and has started to have nightmares about this. Michael, Bill's 16-year-old great-grandson, visits him once or twice a week. Jenna, a social care student on placement, noticed that when Michael arrived to visit his grandfather today he sneaked up behind Bill and whispered something in his ear. Bill then became very distressed and started calling out. Before he left, Jenna asked Michael what he had whispered to his great grandfather. Michael looked a little guilty and said 'Nothing really. I say "the Germans are coming" and he gets a bit excited, that's all.'

1. Is Michael abusing his grandfather? If so, what type of abuse is this? If not, suggest reasons why this behaviour is not abusive.

2. Do you think that Jenna should report the incident and Michael's explanation to anyone else?

3. What do you think should happen next as a response to this situation?

Statistics compiled by Action on Elder Abuse indicate that abuse of elderly people occurs mostly in the family home (64 per cent), followed by residential care (23 per cent), and then in hospital settings (5 per cent).

Indicators of financial abuse

Financial abuse can take many forms but usually involves theft, misuse or manipulation of another person's money, possessions or other financial resources. The signs and symptoms include:

- a sudden, unexplained inability to pay bills

- a reluctance to spend (even when money should not be a problem)

- no food in the house
- unexplained withdrawals from an individual's bank accounts
- money, chequebooks, bank cards, credit cards or possessions going missing
- being under pressure to change the terms of a will
- other people showing an unusual interest in an individual's money or property (assets).

Indicators of institutional abuse

Institutional abuse occurs when the policies of, or the ways of working in, a care setting add to the risk of abuse rather than safeguarding people against it. For example, an organisation might force everyone to accept the same fixed care routines. A manager might say 'that's just how things are' when a social care worker or individual questions how things are done.

The signs and symptoms include:

- rigid routines (such as mealtimes and bed times) or inflexible visiting times
- activities arranged solely for the convenience of staff and the organisation
- cultural or religious needs not being met
- restricting access to food and drink, toilet or baths
- misuse of medication, for example the overuse of sedation to help staff rather than the individual
- lack of privacy, dignity or respect
- restricting access to medical or social care
- examples of poor professional standards and behaviour.

Think about your individuals.

How involved are they in making decisions about their support?

Is your service flexible about meeting individual preferences for mealtimes, bedtimes and food choices?

Indicators of self-neglect

Self-neglect can be accidental or deliberate. An individual who is confused or who has memory problems may neglect themselves unintentionally.

The signs and symptoms include a person:

- neglecting personal hygiene
- not seeking medical or social care
- not taking prescribed medication
- overeating or not eating at all
- self-harming, for example misusing alcohol or illegal drugs or cutting themselves
- not taking exercise
- living in unhygienic conditions that are a risk to health, for example the presence of vermin.

Indicators of neglect by others

Neglect can be passive or active: it may include a lack of attention, abandonment or confinement by family or society.

The signs and symptoms include:

- denial of access to or withholding of health or social care
- denial of individual rights and choices
- withholding medication
- isolating the individual by denying others access to them
- failure to meet the individual's physical, emotional, social, cultural, intellectual or spiritual needs
- failure to provide adequate food, drink, warmth, shelter and safety
- failure in the 'duty of care'
- exposing the individual to risks and dangers.

Factors contributing to vulnerability

An adult in need of safeguarding may be more vulnerable to abuse or neglect because of a variety of factors.

Factors related to the individual who is vulnerable to abuse	Factors related to the situation or care giver that might cause abuse
• Age (young or old) • Isolation • Physical ability or illness creating dependency • Mental and emotional health issues, e.g. dementia, depression, stress • Communication problems, e.g. speech or hearing impairments or learning disability • Behavioural changes, e.g. following a stroke or head injury • Where violence is seen as normal within the environment or relationships • Past history of accusations • Culture or religion • Financial factors	• Prejudice or hostility towards the vulnerable individual • High stress levels or lack of support for the care giver • Care giver is drug or alcohol-dependent, or has physical or mental health issues • Care giver has previously been abused themselves • Lack of understanding about the individual's medical or emotional condition • Lack of leadership and clear roles, responsibilities, policies and procedures • Lack of training or poor monitoring of care provision • Staff shortages

Factors contributing to vulnerability to abuse

Vulnerable people need to be protected from abuse

Case study

In Practice

Mrs Porter is an 83-year-old woman who lives alone. Her health and memory have deteriorated since her husband died two years ago. She has no other family. Mrs Porter receives two visits a day to provide personal care and support at mealtimes.

You haven't visited for two weeks and you are covering as the usual carer is off. You are worried when you see Mrs Porter. She has lost weight, her hair and clothes are dirty, and she seems frightened. When you move towards her, she puts her arms up in front of her face. When you ask if she would prefer a wash or a shower, she says the usual carer doesn't bother. When you undress her, you are shocked to find her body is covered in bruises. When you ask about the bruising, Mrs Porter starts crying: 'I don't like him! He hurts me.' She then tells you that 'he' is the male carer. You then find there's little food in the fridge and cupboards, even though shopping is part of Mrs Porter's care package.

1. What signs and symptoms lead you to suspect Mrs Porter is being abused?

2. What types of abuse are taking place?

3. What factors have made Mrs Porter vulnerable to abuse?

Elderly people can be vulnerable to abuse

4.2 Responding to suspected or alleged abuse

Your questions answered

What should I do if I suspect abuse?

If you suspect abuse you must:

- always report your suspicions

- follow the agreed procedures of your employer

- not be persuaded by others that it is 'unimportant' or 'minor'

- seek advice from the Designated Safeguarding Officer (DSO)

- maintain confidentiality and do not speak about the matter publicly

- keep the individual safe

- remember that you have a duty of care and a **moral** responsibility to act.

Moral Describes behaving in a way that is good and appropriate.

Key Term

Some incidents of abuse or neglect may seem minor, but when they are linked together they may form a pattern which suggests that abuse is happening. So, if in doubt, always report it.

Reporting a manager or colleague, or a family member or carer of the individual is a very sensitive matter. Always treat this as a professional not a personal issue. If you do nothing, you may allow abuse to continue.

If you suspect abuse you should **not**:

- ignore it or hide it for fear of the consequences
- **collude** with colleagues or make the situation worse by covering up for others
- jump to conclusions without examining the facts
- confront the person you think is responsible for the abuse
- leave the individual in an unsafe situation or without appropriate support
- destroy anything that might be needed as evidence.

find out!

Do you know where to find the *Safeguarding Adults at Risk* policies and procedures in your work setting? Find out what they say, so you understand what actions to take if you suspect an individual is being abused or if an individual tells you they are being abused.

Always report suspected abuse

How to preserve evidence of abuse

You must try to preserve any evidence if you think a criminal offence may have taken place.

Do not:

- move or remove anything from a situation where you suspect or observe abuse
- touch anything, unless you have to make the area or person safe
- clean or tidy up
- allow access to anyone not involved in investigating.

Do:

- record any visible signs of abuse, such as bruising, physical injuries or torn clothing

- avoid touching people or objects wherever possible and do not destroy fingerprints

- preserve clothing, footwear, bedding and similar items, and keep them safe and dry

- record any injuries

- preserve and record the state of the individual and the alleged abuser's clothing, and the condition and attitudes of the people involved

- preserve items in a clean paper bag or unsealed envelope

- preserve liquids in clean glasses.

find out!

Find out more about how to make and securely store confidential records of abuse, such as witness statements, reports, photos and any other evidence.

Case study

In Practice

Paul Heston is a 25-year-old man with learning disabilities. He travels to the day centre by bus from his home where he lives with his parents. Paul arrives late one morning, distressed and dishevelled. His coat is torn and muddy. He has a cut on his cheek and facial bruising. He is limping and holding his side. His rucksack, phone and wallet are missing. He says he was attacked by a group of boys after getting off the bus. They dragged him into the nearby park, where they hit, kicked and punched him. They called him names and swore at him. They then stole his wallet and mobile phone. Paul asked a passer-by for help, but no one came to his aid. He is frightened that his father will be angry with him as his phone is new.

1. What would you do in this situation?

2. Which other agencies are likely to be involved in supporting Paul?

3. How would you preserve any evidence?

4.3 National and local policies and local systems for safeguarding

find out !

Does your workplace have a copy of *No Secrets*? Find out if individuals using your service are given information about *Safeguarding Adults at Risk* procedures. If not, why not?

Two key documents that relate to adults in need of safeguarding are:

● *No Secrets* (2000) – guidance on developing and implementing multi-agency policies and procedures to protect vulnerable adults from abuse

● *Safeguarding Adults* (2009) – a national framework of standards for good practice and outcomes in adult protection work.

The table below summarises national legislation with regard to safeguarding.

Legislation or national policy	Summary of key points
Legal powers to intervene	A range of laws enable abusers to be prosecuted, including: • Offences Against the Person Act (1861) – relates to physical abuse • Sexual Offences Act (2003) – relates to sexual abuse • Protection from Harassment Act (1997) – relates to psychological abuse • Section 47 of the National Assistance Act (1948) – relates to neglect.
Human Rights Act (1998)	All individuals have the right to live free from violence and abuse. Rights include: • Article 2: The right to life • Article 3: Freedom from torture (including humiliating and degrading treatment) • Article 8: The right to family life.
Mental Capacity Act (2005)	Outlines five key principles to protect adults at risk who are unable to make their own decisions. Also covers financial abuse.
Safeguarding Vulnerable Groups Act (2006)	Resulted from the Bichard Inquiry in 2002 into the Soham murders and led to the creation of the Independent Safeguarding Authority (ISA) which oversees the vetting and barring scheme.
Health and Social Care (HSC) Act (2008); HSC Act (2010); CQC Regulations (2009)	Established the Care Quality Commission (CQC) to replace National Minimum Standards, and introduced essential standards of quality and safety.

National legislation and safeguarding adults

What roles do different agencies play in adult safeguarding?

The table below identifies a number of different agencies involved in adult safeguarding and outlines their particular roles and responsibilities.

Agency	Key responsibilities
Local authority adult social care services	These agencies: • receive safeguarding alerts • undertake any intervention required to keep individuals safe • liaise/coordinate between all individuals and agencies involved • arrange and record meetings and case conferences • remove the alleged abuser, if required • are represented at police interviews.
All agencies, including: the police, NHS, GPs, medical services, councils, emergency services, independent, voluntary services and charities, private providers, Trading Standards, CQC	These agencies: • work to agreed safeguarding adults policies and procedures • ensure all staff receive regular information about safeguarding training, understand policies and procedures and can recognise signs of abuse • ensure all employees are CRB checked and registered with the ISA prior to employment • inform the ISA of anyone who is unsuitable to work with adults at risk.
The following have additional roles and responsibilities:	
Police	The police: • investigate allegations of abuse if a crime is suspected • gather evidence and pursue criminal proceedings if appropriate • protect people in vulnerable situations.
Medical services, e.g. GP, NHS Acute Trusts	These services: • provide immediate treatment if required • undertake evidential investigations or medical examinations.

Roles and responsibilities of safeguarding agencies

What reports are available regarding serious failures in safeguarding adults at risk?

As a social care worker, you should understand and learn from the findings and recommendations of inquiries into failures in safeguarding practice. In the past few years there have been a number of these, which have been documented in inquiries and serious case reviews, including:

- Margaret Panting Serious Case Review (2004)
- Steven Hoskin Serious Case Review (2007)
- Michael Gilbert Serious Case Review (2011))

The review findings in each case indicated that:

- the fundamental safeguarding needs of each individual were consistently neglected by health, social care and criminal justice agencies
- staff employed by various agencies ignored or failed to recognise the individual's rights and need for protection
- poor communication, planning, coordination and thoughtlessness left each individual in an abusive and dangerous situation
- lack of coordination, information-sharing and integration between agencies resulted in the safeguarding needs of vulnerable individuals being overlooked or neglected.

think about

Use the internet to locate one of the Serious Case Reviews mentioned on this page. Read through the key points and findings.

How were the individuals abused?

What types of abuse did they experience?

Who else do you think was abused?

Could similar failures and abuses happen in your work setting?

Your role in safeguarding and protecting against abuse

There are various different sources of information and advice on your role in the safeguarding and protection of the individuals you support and care for.

As well as your workplace's policy documents, you should have training, updates and regular supervision sessions on types, signs and symptoms of abuse. These should help to give you confidence in your ability to perform this important part of your social care role.

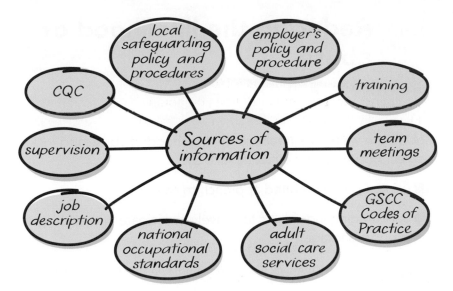

Sources of information and advice about your role in safeguarding vulnerable individuals

REED
SOCIAL CARE

Safeguarding – Coventry City Council

Safeguarding is everyone's responsibility, from relatives and carers to directors and inspectors. If you view safeguarding as a jigsaw, you can see that each individual needs to report and record their accurate information in order to form a full picture. It is therefore essential that our employees take safeguarding seriously to provide a full picture which could prove to be key in the safeguarding of our individuals.

Coventry City Council

@work

4.4 Reducing the likelihood of abuse

Social care workers can reduce the likelihood of abuse and neglect occurring in their workplace by:

- using a person-centred approach to care
- encouraging individuals to actively participate in their care or support package
- allowing individuals in the care setting to make their own choices
- encouraging individuals to make use of accessible complaints procedures
- recognising and reporting unsafe practices.

Person-centred approaches

Person-centred approaches are particularly effective when supporting adults with learning disabilities, adults with mental health problems and individuals with dementia. Every individual has their own unique and different life story, needs, wishes and values. It is important to understand these as a way of putting the person at the centre of the care planning and delivery process. Person-centred approaches are covered in detail in Unit 7.

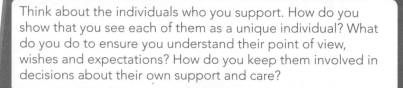

think about

Think about the individuals who you support. How do you show that you see each of them as a unique individual? What do you do to ensure you understand their point of view, wishes and expectations? How do you keep them involved in decisions about their own support and care?

Encouraging active participation

The main result of 'active participation' is the empowerment of the individual concerned. The individual is given independence, and is empowered to make choices about how their personal support or assistance package is delivered. The individual can then *actively* take part in their own care, instead of just *passively* receiving support in a way that is convenient to the provider. Self-directed budgets, where individuals manage their own care package, are an important part of active participation.

It is important to encourage individuals to actively take part in their care

Promoting choices and rights

You can play an active part in promoting the choices and rights of the people you provide care or support for by spending time getting to know each person as an individual. If you get to know them, you can:

- understand their needs and abilities, like and dislikes
- understand how their condition affects their day-to-day life and activities
- understand what is important to them and what their priorities are
- understand how their past experiences impact on their views and current situation
- respect their uniqueness and personal values.

Encouraging use of accessible complaints procedures

Complaints are a very important form of feedback. Being open to feedback means that a social care organisation can review and improve its procedures for the detection of abuse. Social care organisations must develop complaint procedures that are accessible, easy to understand and user-friendly. Individuals and their families should feel able to make complaints without fear of retribution. Accessible complaints procedures should:

- be written in plain English and available in different formats – in pictures, other languages, audio or Braille

Empowerment
Gaining more control over your life by having opportunities to develop greater self-confidence and self-esteem.

Retribution
Something done to injure, punish or 'get back' at someone.

Plain English
Communication styles that are clear, brief and to the point and avoid technical language, particularly in relation to official communication.

Key Terms

- include an explanation of how to use the complaints procedure

- include a way of checking that individuals understand the procedure

- be displayed in public areas of the service

- be provided by staff trained to respond positively to complaints

- encourage individuals to complain if they are dissatisfied with their support

- use a key worker system to ensure individuals are listened to and given the opportunity to complain informally

- confidentially inform individuals using the service when their complaints have been dealt with and what the outcomes are.

4.5 Recognising and reporting unsafe practices

Unsafe practice
An approach or standard of care that puts individuals at risk.

Key Term

Any practice that puts an individual or care worker at risk could be considered unsafe. **Unsafe practice** includes not wearing personal protective equipment, not undertaking risk assessments and ignoring strategies to manage risk. Unsafe practice can also result from insufficient resources (lack of equipment, lack of time or lack of staff) and operational difficulties (lack of training, poor leadership or lack of staff supervision).

What action should you take if you identify unsafe practices?

You have a duty of care to tell your employer about any unsafe practices and to take action to protect yourself and others. You should:

- make any hazardous situation safe where it is possible to do so (for example, use a hazard sign to identify an unsafe environment)

- ensure others are aware of the potential danger – if appropriate, remove and label broken equipment

- report the situation verbally and in writing without delay to the person in charge, completing any incident or maintenance forms that are used in the workplace

- follow up to check if the situation has been dealt with effectively.

Safety is everyone's responsibility in social care settings. In some situations unsafe practices may have become accepted over time, but as a social care worker you should not accept this as 'normal'. You could lose your job if you ignore abuse or don't follow the correct procedure.

Remember to check local procedures, seek advice and, if necessary, register a complaint if you have concerns about apparently unsafe practices. Doing nothing will only support the unsafe practice.

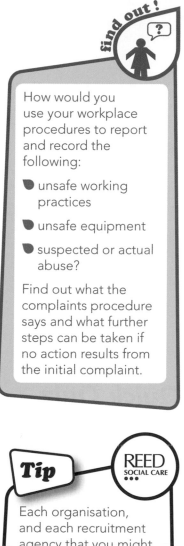

Make a hazardous situation safe where possible

find out! ?

How would you use your workplace procedures to report and record the following:

- unsafe working practices

- unsafe equipment

- suspected or actual abuse?

Find out what the complaints procedure says and what further steps can be taken if no action results from the initial complaint.

Tip   REED SOCIAL CARE •••

Each organisation, and each recruitment agency that you might work for, will have their own safeguarding and whistle blowing policy. You should familiarise yourself with these policies to ensure that you can follow the correct procedure if you ever need to.

What action should you take if there has been no response to reported suspected abuse or unsafe practices?

When you raise a concern and report either suspected abuse or unsafe practices, you should always ensure that you put this in writing. This will allow you to produce detailed, written evidence when your complaint is investigated.

Most complaints procedures include agreed timescales and steps for dealing with a complaint or incident. If you raise concerns about unsafe practices, or report an incident, but the proper timescale for responding to your complaint is not followed, then you should follow your organisation's procedures for grievances. This grievance procedure may involve reporting the situation to a more senior person within the organisation, to the Adult Social Care Services department of your local authority or to the Care Quality Commission (CQC). Depending on the grievance, you may also want to contact your trade union for information and advice.

Quick Quiz

1 Max, a learning disabled man, alleges that one of your female colleagues often strokes and fondles him inappropriately while disguising this as helping him to wash. What should you do?
   a. Reassure Max that your colleague was carefully vetted before being employed.
   b. Phone 999 and report the matter to the police.
   c. Ask Max to describe what happened and report this to your manager.
   d. Make a joke and tell Max to forget it happened.

2 If you suspect that a social care client is being abused in any way, you should:
   a. keep a file, gathering information together until you have a strong case against the perpetrator
   b. inform a senior member of staff, or the person with safeguarding responsibility as soon as possible
   c. avoid working with the client in case they accuse you of being involved in the abuse
   d. confront the alleged abuser and let them know you are watching and will report them if necessary.

3 A colleague tells you a female client has accused another colleague, who is a good friend of yours, of slapping her for swearing. What should you do?
   a. Speak to the client to find out more about the situation.
   b. Advise your colleague to report the matter immediately to a manager or to the person with safeguarding responsibility.
   c. Avoid the client as she may hit out again.
   d. Gather your colleagues in the staffroom to discuss the matter in depth.

4 Eleni is a community support worker in a dementia care team. When she knocks on the door at the home of her 80-year-old client Ena she is alarmed to hear raised voices, a scream and sobbing. Despite waiting for five minutes and knocking again, nobody answers the door. What should Eleni do?
   a. Phone 999 for emergency services.
   b. Phone her manager for advice.
   c. Report the matter to the Care Quality Commission.
   d. Leave a note saying she will come back later to check everything is OK.

Quick Quiz (continued)

5   A client you care for in her own home has Down's syndrome and tells you to take money from her purse to pay for her shopping. Later, her mother accuses you of stealing money from her daughter. What should you do?

   a. Tell the client's mother to call the police if she wants, because you know you have done nothing wrong.

   b. Suggest to the client's mother that you call your manager immediately so you can all discuss her concerns about the missing money together.

   c. Leave the house at once and write up your account of the incident when you get back to the office.

   d. Say that you are angry and insulted by her accusation that you steal from your clients.

6   A social care worker who encourages and supports a client's active participation in their own care and support is:

   a. empowering the individual to take control of their own life

   b. reducing their own workload

   c. giving the individual greater responsibility

   d. taking a risk that needs to be carefully managed.

7   Which of the following care strategies reduces the likelihood of abuse or neglect occurring in a social care workplace?

   a. Using a person-centred approach.

   b. Encouraging active participation of individuals in their care.

   c. Recognising and reporting unsafe practices.

   d. All of the above.

8   Dee is a youth support worker on a local estate. Several of the young people (aged under 18) who attend her 'healthy choices' group are holding a party at the youth centre this evening. One of them gives Dee some cash and asks her to buy alcohol for them from the local off licence. What should Dee do?

   a. Explain that she needs to check first what the guidelines are for having alcohol on the premises.

   b. Refuse to buy alcohol and report the matter to her manager.

   c. Go to the off licence and buy soft drinks and low-alcohol products.

   d. Do as they ask because it will be a really good way to gain their trust.

9   A young woman with learning difficulties that you work with in a community living home has formed a close bond with you, but is now becoming increasingly physical, giving you hugs and asking about your personal life. You think she is sexually attracted to you. What should you do?

   a. Let her down gently by explaining that you have a partner, but that you think she's very attractive and will soon find someone else.

   b. Tell her very forcefully that you don't fancy her at all and that as a staff member you would never go out with a resident.

   c. Return her affection and try to remain good friends with her.

   d. Ask for the advice and support of a supervisor or manager about how to handle the situation with sensitivity.

10   A new community care worker visits a client at home only to find the necessary PPE of gloves and aprons have run out. What should she do?

   a. Work without gloves and an apron, making sure she washes her hands before and after any personal care procedures.

   b. Call her manager to inform her of the situation and seek her advice as to how to proceed.

   c. Explain to the client that it is illegal for her to work without PPE and go on to the next individual on her schedule.

   d. Use the client's own washing up gloves and cooking apron.

Unit 6

Understand the role of the social care worker

This unit will introduce you to the knowledge and skills needed to understand working relationships in social care settings. It will also look at the importance of working in ways that are agreed between you and your social care employer and of working in partnership with others in the social care sector.

Effective and appropriate relationships are central to the role of social care workers. As a social care worker you will need to become skilled at forming and maintaining work relationships with a variety of other people, including individuals, their family members, colleagues and other health and social care professionals. Effective social care workers do not confuse working relationships with friendships or other types of relationship that they have.

On completion of this unit you should:

- understand working relationships in social care settings
- understand the importance of working in ways that are agreed with your employer
- understand the importance of working in partnership with others

6.1 Understanding working relationships in social care settings

Social care workers are employed in a variety of different settings. In every social care setting the ability to form and maintain effective working relationships with clients, their carers, families and partners, as well as with colleagues, managers and other care providers, is central to everyday work activities.

You will need to use your relationship-building skills to provide support and assistance to others and to work co-operatively and effectively with a range of other people. At first glance this might just seem like common sense. However, it requires skill and will improve as you develop your knowledge and experience of social care practice.

did you know?

There are approximately 1.5 million social care workers in the UK workforce. This number is expected to grow significantly over the next 15 years.

Different types of relationships

Experienced and skilled social care workers understand that they have several different types of relationship with others. These include:

- family relationships with parents, brothers, sisters and other relatives
- friendships
- close, personal, romantic and intimate relationships
- working relationships.

Each type of relationship serves a different purpose and meets different needs, both for you and for the other people involved. The expectations, rules and relationship boundaries that apply to your friendships are not the same as those that apply to your work relationships. The distinction between work-based and other personal relationships is particularly important in social care work.

find out!

What different kinds of relationships do you have in your life? Which ones are most important to you? Which ones have most influence on your life?

Tip

You might provide informal care to friends or family throughout your life. Examples of this can be useful to prospective employers – remember to make a note of examples of this kind of care to provide in an interview situation.

Understanding personal relationships

The personal relationships of social care workers are likely to include relationships with others who are family members, friends or a partner with whom you have a close personal, romantic or intimate relationship. Each of these relationships can be classed as a non-work relationship, although they are also different from each other.

Family relationships

Family relationships tend to be based on a deep emotional bond that gives a person a lasting sense of belonging and security. In fact, a baby's first relationship with his or her parents or main care giver is called the **attachment relationship**. It is through this relationship that people learn to feel loved and secure. An effective attachment relationship is necessary for a person to develop a sense of emotional security and confidence.

People aged between 35 and 54 spend most days or every day with their family. People aged between 16 and 24 spend the least time with family members.
(Office for National Statistics, 2011).

Key Terms

Attachment relationship A relationship that is based on strong emotional bonds.

Socialisation The way in which a person learns about the world around them, and the values and expectations of the society they live in.

It is through family relationships that people tend to learn about attitudes and values, develop communication and social skills and work out how to provide care and support for others. This is known as **socialisation**. Family relationships also tend to have a strong influence on a person's self-esteem and self-concept (how they feel about themselves).

A person's early relationships in childhood are thought to provide a model (or 'blueprint') for the relationships they have later in their life. Why might it be important for social care workers to understand this?

Early family relationships have a lasting impact on your life

Friendships

The bonds of friendship are different from the bonds people form through family relationships. They tend to be based on liking another person who you connect with and who has similar attitudes, values and interests to your own.

Friends may feel they have a strong emotional connection to each other. But it is always possible to choose who you spend your time with and change your friends if they don't meet your needs or are no longer fun to be with. Family relationships, on the other hand, are more permanent, less voluntary and more deeply rooted. Ultimately a friendship should help to boost your self-esteem and confidence and contribute positively to the way you feel about yourself as a person.

Friendships play an important part in a person's social and emotional development. They provide you with your first relationships outside the family and require you to give as well as receive social and emotional support. Throughout your life, friends help to shape who you are, what you feel and how you relate to others: they affect your personality, social skills and emotional development.

Friendships support you, make you feel that you are liked and wanted and help to provide a feeling of belonging. Friendships are based on emotional bonds but are better thought of as relationships that connect everyone to a social group.

According to data collected by the Office for National Statistics in 2011, 68 per cent of people aged 16–24 spend most days or every day with friends.

Close personal, romantic and intimate relationships

People usually become interested in close personal, romantic and intimate relationships in their early teens. As teenagers or adolescents, individuals can fall in and out of love quickly. Becoming romantically involved with another person can feel exciting and helps to make you feel good about yourself. Being rejected, or not having your feelings returned, can be painful, but it is a good way to learn more about yourself and what you are looking for in a relationship.

Close personal, romantic and intimate relationships tend to be more emotionally intense and physically intimate than friendships. The emotional and physical boundaries of these relationships are significantly different from those of other friendships and family relationships. These relationships tend to require a greater degree of personal trust and emotional commitment than friendships or work-based relationships.

Case study

In Practice

Bina is a 22-year-old social care worker, employed by a local authority. She currently supports older people living in the community but is a bit bored with her job. She has recently told a colleague that 'it's all old ladies, mashed food and lost handbags'. Bina is keen to apply for a support worker post at a local night shelter for homeless people. She told her colleague, 'At least the users are more my age and some of the *Big Issue* blokes are quite … well … quite nice, aren't they!'

1. What do you think about Bina's motives for applying for the post she is interested in?

2. What might you say to Bina about relationship boundaries as a way of reminding her of the social care worker role?

Tip

Prospective employers will always want to know 'why' you wish to join their organisation, and why you want the role you have applied for. You should think about and discuss your motives for applying for a job with your friends and family prior to the interview process.

Working relationships

Working relationships are different from the different kinds of personal relationships. The main difference is that they are not personal: they are all about working together with others to achieve tasks or goals in an organisation. Most working relationships are between people at different levels and have clear boundaries and dividing lines. The boundaries between different workers are set out in each person's job description and in the arrangements for line managements (who reports to who). This means that workers have different levels of power, authority and responsibility in working relationships. For example, as a social care worker you may have working relationships with:

- your employer, supervisor and manager

- your colleagues or co-workers

- other members of a social care team

- workers from different professional backgrounds

- the partner and family of the individual receiving care, assistance or support.

Effective working relationships are usually based on clear communication, trust and respect between the people involved. Some of the qualities of working relationships are shown in the diagram below.

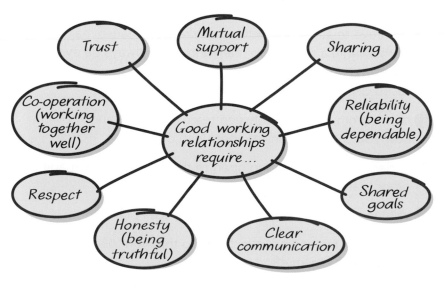

Elements of good working relationships

Just over nine out of ten (91 per cent) UK workers reported that they were satisfied with their working relationships. This is slightly higher than the 87 per cent satisfaction rating of workers in the rest of Europe.

Tip | REED SOCIAL CARE

You will often have more of these qualities than you may realise. Remember to sell yourself to your employer at interview – these skills are just as important as other practical skills that you may have.

What would you do?

If you were at an interview for a social care worker job, which of the qualities or skills listed in the diagram opposite could you say you currently have or are able to contribute to teamwork situations?

Employer/employee relationships

You have a **formal relationship** with your employer. This means that the relationship is based on agreed rules and expectations about how both sides should work together. In particular, an employer has the power to manage the work-related activities of their employees. In turn, employees are expected to understand, accept and carry out the agreed ways of working in their workplace.

Your manager or supervisor is the person who represents the interests of your employer. Your employment contract, as well as the policies and procedures of your workplace, should clearly set out the expectations, rules and boundaries of your relationships with your employer, manager and supervisors.

Relationships with co-workers (colleagues)

In a workplace employment relations survey (ONS, 2011), 60 per cent of employees rated their relations with management as 'good' or 'very good'.

As a social care worker, you will need to form good relationships with your co-workers (or colleagues), as you are likely to work in a care team or multi-agency partnership. Trust, support and co-operating with your co-workers are important aspects of teamwork situations. In social care settings, teams can change quite quickly, as people leave or join, so it is also important to be adaptable, accepting and supportive of co-workers in order to maintain high standards of care provision for individuals.

Being liked, supported and valued by your colleagues will have a positive effect on you. A lack of respectful, effective or co-operative relationships with co-workers can cause major problems within a social care team and must always be avoided or addressed quickly when it occurs. Effective teamwork tends to be based on:

- clear communication between team members and knowing how you can communicate best with others

- understanding and being open to the contributions made by other team members

- valuing and being open to the differences of others

- carrying out your work effectively so that you 'play your part' in the overall team effort.

Relationships between co-workers should be supportive. The best way to make this happen is to look out for others and notice when they are:

- feeling stressed or worried by work or personal problems

- performing their work effectively

- under pressure and having difficulty coping with their workload.

Effective social care teams are made up of co-workers who are supportive of each other. This means sharing information, showing new or less experienced colleagues how to do things and helping out when your co-workers are under pressure or need help. If you help others, they are more likely to help you too – this is mutual support!

Mutual support helps everyone to do a better job

find out !

Who are the most supportive people in your workplace? Think about why these people are more supportive than others. Why do you think they act in this supportive way?

Professional relationships with others

Social care workers have contact with a range of other people in the workplace who are not their manager, supervisor or co-workers. These include people who provide specialist care (for example, nurses, psychologists, speech and language therapists or doctors) or support (for example, teachers, legal advocates or housing staff) for individuals. A social care worker may also have contact with the families of the individuals they work with.

You must manage each of these relationships in a professional way, so that others are confident in your ability to work within the agreed guidelines of your role and to focus on the needs, wishes and preferences of the individuals you provide care or support for.

The qualities needed for effective teamwork always apply to these working relationships. You should always focus on the care-giving goals and the agreed boundaries and limitations of your work role when responding to or providing assistance for other care professionals and the relatives of those receiving care and support.

6.2 Working in ways agreed with your employer

The working relationships that you have with others in your social care setting are strongly influenced by your job or work role. This will be defined by your job description, which explains:

- the responsibilities of your job

- who will supervise you and who you report to (line management)

- the nature of the setting where you work

- any other supervisory responsibilities or managerial aspects of your work role.

Adhering to the scope of the job role

Your job description forms part of your contract of employment. When you sign this contract you accept:

- the responsibilities that go with your work role

- that you will work in ways that have been agreed with your employer

- that you will abide by the laws, codes of practice and regulations that apply to social care settings.

Tip

Ensure that you ask questions about the job description at interview, so that you understand fully what you will be required to do on a day-to-day basis. Not only will this ensure that you make an informed decision about whether to take a job, but it demonstrates an interest in the position to your prospective employer.

find out!

Do you know what your job description says about your work role? When was the last time you actually looked at it? Have a look at it now and think about whether your job description actually describes what you do in your workplace.

Role boundaries, limitations and accountability

Your job description and contract of employment define the boundaries and limitations of your work role as well as your duties and responsibilities. When you sign your contract you are agreeing to work within the scope of your job role. This is important because your employer (and co-workers) will assume that you will make a professional commitment to do your job to the best of your ability and that you will not go beyond what is expected and what you have been trained to do.

You have a defined work role because your employer needs you to carry out particular work activities in your work setting, contributing, alongside colleagues, to the overall work goals of your social care organisation. Effective care provision depends on each person understanding their professional boundaries and working within their professional limitations.

Once you have completed your induction, your employer will hold you **accountable** for the effective performance of your work role. That means you will be expected to carry out your job description and to provide care and support of the expected standard for individuals. Sometimes your manager may need you to take on extra tasks, but you should always make sure that you are able, qualified and experienced to do the work.

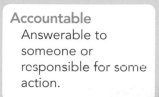

Accountable
Answerable to someone or responsible for some action.

Key Term

How will your employer assess your work performance? Find out about the appraisal system used in your work setting and what you have to do to demonstrate that you are competent and performing to the expected standard.

Agreed ways of working

Your employer will have a range of written policies and procedures about how to provide support, assistance and care in different situations for the individuals who use your care setting or services. These should include clear guidelines on aspects such as the following:

- health and safety
- equal opportunities and inclusion
- confidentiality (keeping things private)
- data protection (keeping information secure)
- supervision
- waste management
- moving and handling
- managing medication
- security and safeguarding.

Each setting has policies and procedures to follow

You should know where to find your organisation's policies and procedures, understand what they say and know how they affect your work role. Policies tend to give general guidance, while procedures give more specific instructions about what to do in defined situations. For example, the moving and handling policy may say 'No manual handling of individuals', whereas the moving and handling procedure should explain in more detail how to use lifting aids or equipment. Following the policies and procedures will ensure that you are working in the safest and most effective way.

Case study

In Practice

Eva is a 46-year-old woman with a long history of mental health problems. She lives alone, has no friends and only sees her brother and sister at Christmas when they visit her flat. Jonathan, a community social care worker, is Eva's new key worker. Officially he should make appointments to see her every fortnight or when she contacts him, but he has started to 'pop in' to see Eva most evenings on his way home from work. Eva likes his company but isn't confident enough to say that he shouldn't come so often.

1. Do you think that Jonathan is adhering to the scope of his job role?

2. Which activities described in the case study are likely to be outside his job description?

3. Explain why Jonathan's approach to supporting Eva may be seen as problematic and inappropriate by his supervisor or managers.

Do you know where to find the policies and procedures in your work setting? When was the last time you looked at them? Can you explain the day-to-day impact of different policies and procedures on your job role?

REED
SOCIAL CARE

Working in ways agreed by your employer – a leading housing organisation

Each of our employees plays an important part in our organisation. The reason we work so well together is because everybody knows what is expected of them and follows these expectations. When people don't do what they have committed to do or they try to do too much, this always leads to problems. While we always look for helpful, committed employees, it is better to report something that you feel needs to be done rather than attempt to do something that you are not trained for or not expected to do.

@work

Multi-agency working is a good way of sharing both resources and expertise

find out!

What different kinds of partnerships are there in your day-to-day work? Think about all the other people you work with and the agencies or organisations who work with your employer's organisation or agency.

Multi-agency working An arrangement where workers from different agencies or organisations work together.

Multi-disciplinary working This is where different care professionals work together in the same team.

Key Terms

6.3 Working in partnership with others

How would you describe your role as a social care worker to someone you have just met? Would you say you 'work with' people or 'do things for' people? In the past, it used to be that you would 'do things for' people in care settings. Now you are expected to work in partnership with the people you support. There are many kinds of partnerships in the social care field, including with:

- co-workers (colleagues)
- practitioners/workers from other agencies
- individuals
- the families and friends of individuals.

Partnerships with individuals

A big part of your role as a social care worker is making sure that people have the support they need to get on with their daily lives. Your relationship with each individual should be based on the idea of partnership – working together in a constructive, helpful and equal way.

Your aim is to support individuals to make their own decisions, if possible, and to do as much as they can for themselves. An effective partnership should allow you to offer and provide more support when it is wanted and needed and less support when it isn't required or desired by the person you are working with.

Teamwork and partnerships

Effective partnership in social care is based on teamwork. Practitioners increasingly work in a range of different groups, known as integrated **multi-agency** and **multi-disciplinary** teams in health and social care settings. This mixed or 'integrated' way of working means that you get people with lots of different skills and specialisms working together to provide high-quality care for individuals. Multi-agency working is a good way of sharing both resources and expertise – and it also saves time and money for service providers.

Tip

REED
SOCIAL CARE
•••

Remember that if you leave an organisation for a new job, your previous employers will be providing a reference for you. It is important to maintain good professional working relationships throughout your career. Also remember that you may find yourself working with – or for – former colleagues again in the future!

find out !
?

Is your care setting a multi-disciplinary or multi-agency environment? Do you come into contact with practitioners with different training backgrounds and areas of expertise? To find out more about how you all work together, you could ask some of the people you work with about their own job roles and skills.

Partnership working within multi-agency teams, and with co-workers or other professionals in a social care setting, requires a clear understanding of, and agreement on, issues such as:

- communication
- sharing information and confidentiality
- decision making procedures
- each practitioner's role and responsibilities
- how to resolve conflicts
- the goals or objectives of a care or support package.

Open communication between team members is vital for effective partnership working. For example, there should always be open and clear discussions about the needs of individual individuals and the shared goal that everyone is trying to achieve. After all, it makes sense to agree on things if you are working in close partnerships.

It is also important to have clear processes for decision making that everyone understands and complies with. If team members are regularly left out of the decision making process, they may come to feel rejected or demotivated. Even where it is the more senior people in an organisation or agency who make decisions, there should be a chance for everyone employed in a social care setting to put forward their opinion. This helps to build stronger feelings of teamworking.

Phil is 26 years old. He has Down's syndrome, depression and has recently been diagnosed with diabetes. Phil likes to be active and attends a local day centre run by a learning disabilities support group. He sees his GP once a fortnight and has a community support worker who meets him every week. Phil's GP has said he will arrange for a specialist nurse to help him to manage his diabetes.

1. Identify the different forms of care that Phil receives.

2. Which care practitioners could be considered members of Phil's 'care team'?

3. How might Phil benefit from a partnership approach to his care?

find out !

Read a care or support plan that has been written for an individual in your setting. Think about the different care workers involved in providing care, support or assistance for the person: how does this plan reflect the differing roles of different practitioners?

Resolving conflicts

When health and social care workers are working closely together in teamwork situations, there can be conflicts or tensions between different practitioners or agencies. Different approaches and views about priorities do occur in care teams. It is important to have clear procedures about how to resolve these situations so that individuals' interests are not affected. Showing respect to other health and social care workers and learning to understand their work roles, professional responsibilities and priorities helps to create and maintain good working relationships in care teams that use a partnership working approach.

Your questions answered

How should I deal with conflict at work?

If you find yourself involved in a dispute or conflict with another care worker, remember that this is about work – it's not a personal argument. You should always keep hold of your own professional standards, even if others are being unhelpful or difficult. Remember, even if you have a very different opinion from someone else, you should communicate clearly and remain polite. As a social care worker you should always:

- value the different skills, input and opinions of others
- acknowledge (or take on board) the efforts and contributions of other people.

The first rule in any situation where there is a conflict of opinion or approach is, of course, that everyone should stay calm and remain professional. The main skills and approaches needed for resolving workplace conflicts include:

- managing your own stress
- remaining calm when under pressure
- being aware of both your own and the other person's verbal and non-verbal communication in a stressful situation
- controlling your own emotions and behaviour
- avoiding threatening others, even when you feel frightened or very angry with them
- paying attention to the feelings being expressed (as well as the words spoken) by the other person
- being aware and respectful of social, cultural and value differences between you and the other person

What would you do?

How do you think you would respond if you ever became involved in a conflict or disagreement with a colleague in your work setting? How would you try to resolve it? Are there any support or advice services that you could use in this kind of situation?

- developing a readiness to forgive and forget
- being specific and clear in the way you communicate
- having the ability to seek compromise
- trying not to exaggerate or over-generalise
- avoiding accusations
- listening to others in an active way.

Accessing support and advice

You may need support or advice about partnership working when it comes to:

- sharing information
- issues of confidentiality
- explanations of roles and responsibilities
- professional boundaries
- understanding agreed ways of working.

You can obtain advice and support on these subjects from different sources. The first step is to talk to your manager, supervisor or senior colleagues. Don't worry about asking others for help: your manager or senior colleagues will see this as a positive, professional step, not as a sign of weakness. When thinking about asking others for information or help in understanding an issue, remember to consider the needs of the people you care for.

You should also look at your organisation's policy documents. These provide written guidance and should give you lots of information on issues relating to partnership and teamworking. You can find support and advice from other places, including:

- mentoring organisations
- independent advisory organisations
- trade unions
- occupational health services (at your workplace).

If you need support, the first step is to talk to your manager

Quick Quiz

1   Which of the following are an example of working relationships?
    a. Sibling relationships
    b. Friendships
    c. Employer/employee relationships
    d. Romantic relationships

2   How are working relationships different from personal relationships?
    a. They involve intimate physical contact.
    b. They are focused on a clear organisational task or goal.
    c. They are always very short-term.
    d. They are more emotionally intense.

3   Which of the following are an example of formal relationships?
    a. Parent and child relationships
    b. Attachment relationships
    c. Relationships with co-workers/colleagues
    d. Marital relationships

4   Working relationships with people employed by other care organisations occur in:
    a. partnerships
    b. multi-agency teams
    c. multi-disciplinary teams
    d. personal care work.

5   The agreed ways of working in a social care setting are outlined in the workplace:
    a. policies
    b. protocols
    c. procedures
    d. all of the above.

6   The scope of a social care worker's role should be outlined in the:
    a. contract of employment
    b. code of conduct
    c. job description
    d. code of practice.

7   Which of the following workplace policies would you consult to find out about agreed ways of working in relation to record keeping?
    a. Health and safety policy
    b. Data protection policy
    c. Security and safeguarding policy
    d. Equal opportunities and inclusion policy

8   Celia, an occupational therapist, Natasha, a social care worker, Davinder, a social worker, and Erin, a housing manager, all work in the same independent living support service. How would you describe their team?
    a. A multi-agency team
    b. A health and social care team
    c. A partnership team
    d. A multi-disciplinary team

9   What is the best response when there is a disagreement about the best approach to take to a care or support situation?
    a. Argue forcefully to get your point across.
    b. Listen, be respectful and seek compromise.
    c. Make a formal written complaint that sets out your position clearly.
    d. Avoid working with the other person to prevent conflict occurring again.

10 Which of the following sources of support and advice about partnership working issues or problems should be available to all social care workers?
    a. A solicitor
    b. An independent advocate
    c. Their supervisor or line manager
    d. A trade union representative

Principles of
communication in
adult social care settings

Everyone communicates every day with their family members, friends and colleagues; many people have worked hard on their personal communication skills in order to create and maintain fulfilling relationships.

In order to contribute effectively to the care your team provides, you will need to develop and use your knowledge and skills in communication.

People who use health and social care services have a variety of special requirements, due to the physical or emotional impact of their illness or disability; or maybe because of language requirements and preferences.

All workers – at all levels – are responsible for communicating effectively, appropriately and accurately with people using health and social care services and with each other in order to provide safe and effective care.

This unit builds on knowledge gained at Level 2 (in Unit 1) of the importance of communication in adult social care settings. It discusses methods of communication that meet the range of needs, wishes and preferences of individuals, and considers ways to overcome communication barriers.

On completion of this unit you should:

- understand why effective communication is important in adult social care settings
- understand how to meet the communication and language needs, wishes and preferences of an individual
- understand how to overcome barriers to communication
- understand principles and practices relating to confidentiality

10.1 Why effective communication is important in adult social care settings

Reasons for communication

Appropriate and effective communication – with individuals, their families and carers, team members, fellow professionals and those in partner organisations – helps to promote people's well-being, and to prevent errors.

Throughout this unit the special communication needs of clients with dementia will be considered.

You may be working in a service which has several patients with dementia; or working with individuals with other conditions who may be starting to experience the early symptoms and effects of dementia. If you work in health and social care, family members, friends and neighbours may ask you about local services for people with dementia.

In Level 2 Unit 1 (page 3) you considered how it would feel to spend a day without using any form of communication, and reflected on how impossible your working life would be without communicating. People communicate for pleasure; to make things happen; to learn and to understand.

In your personal and work life you will communicate to:

- express your needs, wants and feelings
- share experiences
- debate ideas and share information
- ask and answer questions
- reassure and express empathy.

Through communicating in different ways people socialise and build relationships; these are essential to everybody's emotional well-being.

> **did you know?**
>
> Within 20 years the number of people in the UK with dementia is likely to be nearly one million. Many health and social care organisations have started to pay more attention to the special needs of dementia sufferers, and the training needs of staff. The Alzheimer's Society has developed a Dementia Adviser service to provide information, and aims to achieve the best outcome by building relationships with health and social care professionals and reaching out to more people with dementia.

> **did you know?**
>
> About 7 per cent of the impact when you speak comes from the words you say, 38 per cent from the tone of your voice and the rest (55 per cent) from your body language.

Context of communication

Communication takes place in a wide range of different situations and using different media or methods. This could be:

- in your relationships with family, partner and friends

- at work

- as a customer, consumer or as an individual.

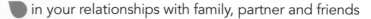

How do you adapt your communication styles for different situations?

- One-to-one – consider the type of relationship you have with the other person and whether you would both be comfortable using non-verbal communication such as touch.

- Group – where there may be competition to be heard and different expectations from group members. Sometimes group communication is in a formal style, such as at a meeting or seminar, where there are conventions about how and when to speak.

- Individuals – being sensitive to the person's own emotional, physical, language and cultural needs; and using our listening skills.

- Children – using age-appropriate language and images without patronising them and being particularly sensitive to their circumstances.

- Professionals/colleagues – abbreviations and may lead to misunderstanding. Complex information needs to be given as accurately and concisely as possible.

Non-verbal communication skills Includes using eye contact; affirmative actions such as nodding; allowing silence and relaxing your body.

Verbal communication skills Includes checking, clarifying, encouraging, reflecting, affirming and summarising.

Key Terms

Listening

Active listening is an essential part of effective communication. Many people only remember less than half of what they hear. Listening is made up of **non-verbal** and **verbal communication skills**.

By practising and improving your listening skills you will be more productive at work and enjoy more rewarding relationships in your home and personal life. You will find that you need to concentrate in order to listen well.

Tip

Listening is as important as speaking in a social care setting – and the same is true at interview. Make sure that you listen to your interviewer rather than simply speaking the lines which you may have rehearsed in advance. You can gain key hints of what a company is looking for from listening to the interviewer.

Listening is an important aspect of communication

How communication affects relationships at work

Effective and happy teams depend on good working relationships between everyone.

Communicating effectively with colleagues and those using your services will help to build trust, avoid misunderstandings and agree responsibilities.

If you use a range of communication methods with individuals, it will help them to expresss their needs and wants; and help you to listen and understand them.

Leadership – a UK housing organisation

Staff should always seek to exhibit leadership skills, regardless of the position that they work in. As you progress in your role, showing leadership skills when working with individuals and with other team members will not only help you in your day-to-day work, but will also help you progress in the future.

@work

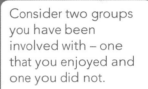

Consider two groups you have been involved with – one that you enjoyed and one you did not.

- What made you want to continue being part of the group or want to leave it?

- What made you feel excited or bored?

- What made you feel involved or left out?

- What about the group leader? Did they make you feel valued? To what extent did they control the group?

Negotiation skills

Negotiation skills are useful to reach agreements about responsibilities and actions where there are conflicting views. You need to be skilful in expressing your expectations and in listening to the other person's responses. Successful negotiation will include some compromise, and lead to agreeing actions that you both accept and carry out.

When negotiating you will need to think about:

- the goals – yours and those of the other person
- what you might trade
- what alternatives there are
- the impact of the negotiation
- the expected outcome
- the potential consequences
- the balance of the relationship
- the possible solutions and compromises.

Tip

REED
SOCIAL CARE

Although negotiation skills will be essential in your career, an interview is not the time to negotiate over salary or other benefits. There is plenty of time for this once you have been offered the job. Don't mention salary unless the interviewer talks about it first.

Negotiation is a useful skill when people disagree

Conflict

Skilfully managing **conflict** can avoid an interaction escalating into an emotional situation. Keeping your emotions under control makes it easier to understand the conflict and resolve the issue. In some circumstances it is best to prevent the conflict if possible; for example, if an emotional outcome would lead to further difficulties such as aggressive behaviour.

You will already have experience of working in a team, a class, or a group. Everyone's communicatiuon skills will contribute to the group achieving its purpose.

What do you know about emotional intelligence?

The book *Emotional Intelligence* by Daniel Goleman explores how our emotions play a significant role in the way we think and make decisions. Emotional intelligence includes being self-aware, controlling impulsive reactions, being motivated and socially acute. It is the basis for successful personal and workplace relationships.

Perhaps the best way of understanding emotional intelligence is to observe a lack of it – for example, in many of the characters in television soaps!

Conflict This can be useful in understanding the other person's worries and needs because it arises from deeply held beliefs.

Key Term

Find out more about Tuckman and Jensen's stages of group development by searching on the internet.

It is useful to know about the different stages of group development.

Tuckman and Jensen (1977) described the stages of group development.

Tuckman and Jensen's stages of group development

10.2 Meeting the communication and language needs, wishes and preferences of an individual

Needs, wishes and preferences of individuals

Building a successful relationship with an individual should start before you first meet them. Part of the initial assessment of the person will include finding out and recording their communication needs:

- their first or preferred language
- their preferred method of communication (for example sign language)
- any additional learning needs
- any physical disabilities.

Five senses The senses used for communication are hearing, sight and touch. The other two are smell and taste.

Key Term

find out!

Alternative methods of communication include:
- a second or alternative language
- British Sign Language
- Makaton
- Braille
- signs, symbols, pictures and writing
- objects of reference
- finger spelling
- communication passports
- human aids to communication such as translators
- technological aids such as hearing aids.

Ask your team leader about how to use some of these methods in practice in the area in which you work, and how to get further support or specific training in using them.

Your questions answered

What are the special communication needs for people with dementia?

Being able to talk to someone is a basic human need and having dementia does not change this.

People with dementia may have memory problems and/or changes in the ways that they experience their surroundings. They may also have other sensory difficulties such as reduced hearing and sight.

People with dementia need particular support with communication. Changes in their understanding and reality sometimes lead to 'challenging' behaviour. They may find it frustratingly difficult to express their needs and staff or carers may misunderstand them – you will need to find out what their behaviour means.

Give the person time to say what they need, and understand that they may be using behaviour as a way of communicating. Sometimes you will need to simplify or rephrase what you have said, and it is often best to speak in short sentences.

Get to know the person with dementia; find out about their preferences, needs and fears – either directly from them or from their loved ones.

When starting an interaction with a client or an individual with dementia, remind them of who you are and explain what you are going to do, leaving time for the person to respond to you.

Tip

Ensure that your CV clearly shows any additional languages that you speak, or your ability to use alternative methods of communication such as sign language. There is increased demand in adult social care for people who have additional communication skills.

Argyle's stages of the communication cycle

Unit 1 looked at communication as a two-way process that can be affected by barriers and distractions or 'noise'. Argyle described communication as a circular process. Barriers or noise may affect any of the stages of Argyle's communication cycle.

In the context of what you have learnt so far in this unit, reflect on a time when you experienced conflict with another person. How was the conflict resolved? Who took responsibility for leading the resolution and what skills did they use to do this?

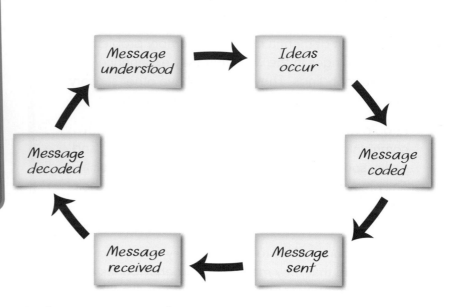

Argyle's communication cycle

Communication methods and styles

Rapport Where two or more people relate well with each other.

Key Term

It is helpful to develop your skills in a range of communication methods. As well as **rapport**, think about using simple signing, symbols and pictures, touch, music and drama, objects of reference and technological aids. Some of these can be particularly useful for people with dementia and others with special communication needs.

Your questions answered

Why is rapport useful?

You may notice that when communication is going well, the people involved have rapport. Rapport will allow two people to argue while staying connected to each other.

Using the skill of rapport is useful in negotiation, interviews, presenting, leading groups and parenting as well as in your work in health and social care – assessesing, planning and reviewing care.

Once you have created rapport with a person, you will start influencing them and they will influence you. The higher the degree of rapport the greater the potential to influence.

What are some tips to get started?

- Mirror elements of the other person's posture, gestures and facial expression.

- Match their voice: their pitch, tone, volume and speed of talking and their natural rhythms.

- Match the other person's use of language, and their way of talking about a subject .

- Match their breathing and general level of energy in a subtle way.

Be careful not to overdo these things.

Responding to reactions

Argyle's Communication Cycle illustrates that, when two people communicate, the person receiving the message will react to the message and the way it was delivered. The emotional state of the person receiving the message will also influence the way they receive and respond to it.

If you are the person sending the message you will need to look for signs that information has been received and understood. You may need to change your communication method in **response** to the other person's reaction to your message. If they react strongly, think about why they received the message in the way that they did. As the person sending the message you will need to find a way of calming things down. Where conflict or strong reactions occur you need to lead the other person to a level where you can reach agreement.

Response
Responses to a message may be verbal – including words used, tone, pitch or even silence; non-verbal – including body language, facial expressions, eye contact, gestures and touch.

Key Term

Your questions answered

What is 'chunking up and down' and how can I use this idea in my work setting?

There are different levels at which everyone communicates, from high-level general principles or abstract ideas through to specific details. This concept was described by Robert Dilts as 'neurological levels'.

Chunking up and down is a useful tool for negotiation and managing conflict. If you continue to explore issues and solutions at a level at which people do not agree, you are unlikely to resolve the issue.

Try to chunk up to a level at which you and the other person agree; then chunk back down to the details, but only at the speed that you both can continue to agree.

To chunk up, use questions such as: What is this an example of? What is the intention?

To chunk down, ask the person questions to get more specific details. Use questions like: What is an example of this? What? Who? Where specifically?

Notice how TV and radio interviewers often use this technique. The interviewee may try to skip over the detail and move to general ideas, or describe a specific story to avoid conflict about principles. A skilled interviewer will lead the interviewee to the level at which the conflict occurs.

Successful chunking contributes to excellent communication skills and it takes practice.

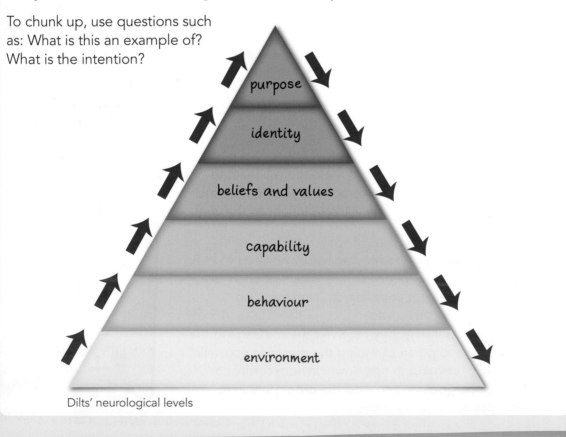

Dilts' neurological levels

10.3 Overcoming barriers to communication

Recognising differences in use and interpretation of communication methods

Both the person sending the message, and the person receiving it, will interpret the message in the context of their background, culture and previous experiences. Age, gender and socio-economic group will affect how the message is interpreted. People tend to relate more easily to those of a similar age and culture, through a shared use of words, intonations, body language, gestures and eye contact. National and international events, films, public figures, music, fashion, 'culture' and traditions also provide a common ground. So when communicating with a person who is a different age, or from a different cultural background, try to find specific areas that you can share.

In Practice

Spiritual beliefs and traditions

Cherry Tree Care Home is in a large city and people from many faiths and traditions live there. The staff have been educated to respect the value of the residents' spiritual beliefs as it is well understood that practising your beliefs is beneficial to physical and mental health, especially during times of illness and emotional stress.

Residents are offered a wide range of reading materials. They choose what is on television and the radio and what music is played. They are encouraged to have private time with loved ones so that they can communicate affection and love in a way that is meaningful for them and respects their culture.

The values at Cherry Tree have helped the staff develop confidence in talking with the residents about their different faiths. The residents are happy to do this as they appreciate that the staff are genuinely interested in them.

Newer members of staff who may be less confident in having conversations about spiritual beliefs are supported by talking with colleagues, religious leaders and residents' families to learn more.

The atmosphere at Cherry Tree is respectful and inclusive. The residents and their families all feel that they are valued as individuals.

think about …❗

It is what you say… :

- ◗ Use positive language – being optimistic promotes positive feelings in the other person and is more likely to get positive results; it makes you feel better as well. Find a way of saying words such as 'yes', 'create' and 'improve' instead of 'no', 'bad' and 'quit'.

- ◗ Replace 'but' with 'and' – because saying 'but' cancels out what you've just said. Try 'I want to be more healthy, and healthy food is more expensive' instead of 'I want to be more healthy but healthy food is more expensive'. Notice how 'and' can make you feel more likely to think more creatively about trying some new recipes, rather than being negative about the potential costs.

- ◗ Consider the positive impact of expressions such as 'I have lots of experience' rather than 'I feel under-valued'.

- ◗ Take note of attention-grabbing phrases in the media like 'funding slashed', 'torrents of information' and 'mountains of paperwork'.

Tip

REED SOCIAL CARE

These tips are extremely useful to follow when at interview as well as in the workplace. You should ensure that you speak slowly and confidently, and try to build rapport with your interviewer. Try to avoid the barriers to communication (see page 55).

think about …❗

…AND the way that you say it:

- ◗ Speak slowly – it makes it easier for the other person to understand what you are saying and that has much more impact.

- ◗ Speak confidently – practise words beforehand. Remember compliments and how they make you feel. Then remember them when you need to say something important.

- ◗ Mirroring the way the other person speaks and their language (within reason) helps to build rapport.

- ◗ Repeating what someone has said back to them checks your understanding, and can help the other person make sense of what they are saying or understand its impact. Summarising in a more positive way may be helpful.

Barriers to effective communication

In Unit 1, barriers to communication were described as noise that interferes with sending and receiving a message. This is:

- physical (external)
- physiological (biological)
- psychological (assumptions and judgements)
- semantic (confusing words).

Overcoming barriers

You can overcome barriers to communication – look back at the tips on page 11 of Unit 1 (Level 2). You can also try:

- speaking slowly and calmly
- simplifying your language and avoiding jargon
- using pictures and symbols, and getting the person to express themselves in this way
- moving to a quiet, private area
- dealing with the person's main issue first – they may be upset, tired, hungry or in pain
- building rapport with the person.

think about ...!

How else can you overcome communication barriers? Check with your manager about how you can access these in your workplace. For example:

- technological aids such as hearing aids, induction loops, telephone relay services
- human aids such as interpreters, signers, translators.

find out !

What support is available to your organisation to help communication? For example, you could find out more about local interpreting and translation services, speech and language services and support provided by charities such as the Stroke Assocation and Royal National Institute for Deaf People (RNID).

If you think there is a misunderstanding, first check that the person has understood the message. Remember that it is not just about what you say – they, or you, might have misinterpreted body language or other visual cues. You also need to actively listen, and repeat back what you have heard, perhaps in different words.

Remember that the communication barrier may actually be you; and as the person providing the care you are responsible for reducing or removing the barriers.

What would you do?

Leslie lives in the residential home where you work. He has dementia and tends to be withdrawn and unwilling to communicate. This morning Leslie has been tearful and has refused his lunch. Consider the approaches you could take to find out what is wrong.

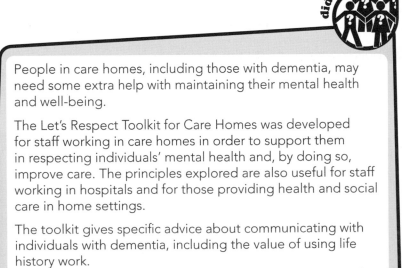

did you know?

People in care homes, including those with dementia, may need some extra help with maintaining their mental health and well-being.

The Let's Respect Toolkit for Care Homes was developed for staff working in care homes in order to support them in respecting individuals' mental health and, by doing so, improve care. The principles explored are also useful for staff working in hospitals and for those providing health and social care in home settings.

The toolkit gives specific advice about communicating with individuals with dementia, including the value of using life history work.

www.nmhdu.org.uk/news/lets-respect-toolkit-for-care-homes-published

10.4 Understanding principles and practices relating to confidentiality

Confidentiality

In Unit 1 (Level 2) you started to explore the principles of **confidentiality** and how these relate to health and social care, including the application of the Data Protection Act.

The principle of 'need to know' is the basis for the security and confidentiality of personal and sensitive information.

Maintaining confidentiality

Information governance rules, processes and training arrangements will be in place in your organisation. These support the requirements of the Data Protection Act (1998) and the business needs of the organisation about respecting confidentiality and communication. Examples include:

- using passwords and 'smart cards' to access computer systems

- preventing the use of memory sticks on computers in the workplace

- storing paper records in locked metal cabinets

- the individual keeping and taking responsibility for their own records (this is commonly done in maternity services)

- asking for the person's permission to look at their record (this is part of the process for using the healthcare Summary Care Record).

Using and handling information in health and social care is covered in more detail in Unit 9 (Level 2) and in Unit 16.

> **Confidentiality** This means keeping information private when it does not need to be shared, or must not be shared.
>
> **Key Term**

Tip

When giving examples at interview, always maintain your current employer's confidentiality – use anonymous examples and do not give away any information that could breach confidentiality legislation.

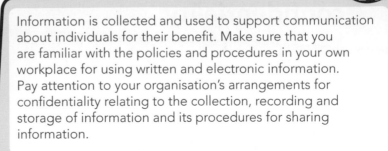

Information is collected and used to support communication about individuals for their benefit. Make sure that you are familiar with the policies and procedures in your own workplace for using written and electronic information. Pay attention to your organisation's arrangements for confidentiality relating to the collection, recording and storage of information and its procedures for sharing information.

Your questions answered

What are Caldicott Guardians?

Dame Fiona Caldicott's report, published in 1997, identified weaknesses in handling confidential patient information in parts of the NHS. In response to the report, Caldicott Guardians were introduced into the NHS, and later to social services and other healthcare organisations.

The Caldicott Guardian is a senior person responsible for protecting the confidentiality of individual and patient information, and enabling appropriate information-sharing. The Caldicott Guardian plays a key role in ensuring that their organisation meets the expected standards for handling identifiable patient information.

Tensions caused by confidentiality

We communicate information about individuals between teams and organisations in order to make it easier for them to use different services. NHS patients usually assume that their information is held by the NHS as a whole; however, you normally need to ask the individual for consent to share their information between organisations.

Sometimes information must be shared without consent; for example to warn of a hazard or to protect someone from harm. Examples of this include abuse, suicidal behaviour or statements indicating plans to kill another person. Again, the concept of 'need to know' is a useful underlying principle here. Individuals and the public expect organisations to have clear and publicised policies for information sharing.

Your questions answered

What is 'whistle-blowing'?

'Whistle-blowing' occurs when a worker communicates a concern about something dangerous or illegal at work that affects others, including individuals and members of the public. It can be described as 'making a disclosure in the public interest'. The disclosure is normally made to the employer or a regulator. A clear policy for raising issues should be in place in your organisation, supporting an open culture. Staff need to feel comfortable raising concerns about patient safety in a responsible way.

This will reduce the risk of serious concerns being mishandled, whether by the employee or by the organisation.

It is important that employees understand that they can raise concerns with their employer without fear of exposure or getting into trouble.

Quick Quiz

1 Semantic 'noise' is one of the four types of distraction or barriers to communication. Which of the following is not an example of semantic 'noise'?

a. Technical expressions

b. Shouting

c. Very long sentences

d. Acronyms

2 Which of the following is not one of the five senses?

a. Smell

b. Thinking

c. Touch

d. Hearing

3 Which of the following is not one of the five stages of group development as described by Tuckman and Jensen in 1977?

a. Joining

b. Storming

c. Norming

d. Adjourning

4 Which of the following is a way to maintain confidentiality in day-to-day communication?

a. Speak loudly and clearly.

b. Avoid using your smart-card.

c. Meet your colleague at a coffee shop in town to discuss an individual's needs.

d. Know who you are speaking with on the telephone.

5 Which of the following is not a primary communication method?

a. Speaking and listening

b. Writing and reading

c. Body language and gestures

d. Braille

6 Which of the following is not an alternative method of communication?

a. A second or alternative language

b. Art and music

c. British Sign Language

d. Signs and symbols

7 Why were Caldicott Guardians introduced in health and social care organisations?

a. They were to guard the entrance of Caldicott hospital.

b. The number of children in care was getting too high.

c. Care homes were going out of business.

d. There were weaknesses in handling confidential patient information in the NHS.

8 When you would share information without consent?

a. If the person is below the age of consent (a child)

b. To warn of suicidal behaviour

c. To share information with the person's bank

d. To tell a GP you think the person needs different medications

9 Which of the following statements about chunking up and down using the neurological levels described by Robert Dilts is not true?

a. It is a useful way of managing negotiation by leading the other person to a 'level' where you agree.

b. It is used by TV and radio interviewers to lead the interviewee to the level at which conflict occurs.

c. It is best to avoid getting into the detail by 'chunking up'.

d. Use expressions like 'what is this an example of?' and 'where specifically did this happen?' to 'chunk down'.

10 Who would you inform of a concern in the context of 'whistle-blowing'?

a. Your immediate supervisor

b. The local newspaper

c. A senior person in the human resources department

d. Your best friend

Principles of personal **development in** adult social care

This unit will help you to understand reflective practice and how this can be utilised to support your personal development in the health and social care sector.

Reflecting or thinking about practice in order to improve tends to ensure that quality standards will be met. Care workers are faced with many changes as national standards, legislation and guidance documents are reviewed. This unit will help you to think about your performance in the light of these changes and to plan how you might improve and develop your practice personally.

On completion of this unit you should:

- understand how to reflect on practice in adult social care
- understand the importance of feedback in improving own practice
- understand how a personal development plan can contribute to own learning and development

11.1 Reflecting on practice in adult social care

What is reflective practice?

Good practice in the health and social care sector arises from a team working together for the benefit of individuals in their care. In the past, staff in this sector may have performed their duties by focusing on separate tasks that needed to be done throughout a setting, such as making all the beds or giving everyone their medications. Now carers and nurses focus on people as individuals, looking after all their needs, so one carer may look after four to six people, making their beds, administering their medication, tending to their hygiene, mobility, general care, nutrition, treatments and respecting their individual preferences.

This 'personalised care' has happened because it was found to benefit individuals. People realised this through a process of reflection, observation, thinking about how things might be done differently, trying it out and thinking again. This process was developed by David Kolb and is known as the 'Experiential Learning Cycle', which involves:

- the experience of doing the job

- thinking about the job, i.e., reflecting and analysing, during the task or afterwards

- devising different ways to do the job or solve the problem, using a new **concept**

- trying out the new ideas and then reflecting again on the success, or not, of the new concept.

This is now called reflective practice and is an ongoing tool for social care workers.

Concept An abstract idea – often thought about through analysis of situations.

Key Term

Tip

If you were unsuccessful at interview, what will you reflect on? How will you judge what to do next time?

Case study

In Practice

Barbara is a carer in a residential setting and has noticed that the home does not provide ear phones or radio in residents' rooms. The residents often look quite bored so she decides to talk with her manager, who agrees to suggest it to the owner. The residents are asked whether they would like radio and ear phones and Barbara will evaluate the success of this intervention.

think about ...!

List four things that you have done differently as a result of reflection. Compare these with a friend and discuss what observations and thoughts prompted the changes you made in your life and how these changes affect the way you think and feel.

Indicate how Barbara experienced the learning cycle by adding a statement for A, B, C and D

A = What is Barbara's experience?

B = How does she reflect on her experience?

C = What is Barbara's new concept?

D = What will Barbara do when the new idea is tried out?

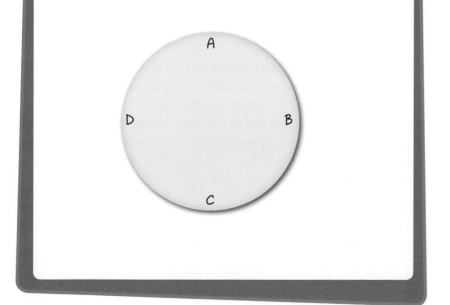

How reflective practice improves the quality of the service

Reflective practice is an ongoing skill and a good habit to develop. If you keep observing how you and colleagues are working for the benefit of the people in your care, you will continuously improve your performance and you will find that you are developing professionally as well as personally.

Alongside this skill, you will need to think about how your practice meets the standards as set out in the **National Minimum Standards, Codes of Practice, the Essential standards of Quality and Safety (2010)**. These are set standards of working that you will find out about during your induction period. You must be aware of them and work to high standards of care. You will also need to be familiar with the policies and procedures of your organisation, such as for health and safety, equality and diversity, safeguarding individuals in your care, your duty of care and preventing and controlling infection.

When you start work you should receive an induction period (introduction to the basic but most important ways of working), followed by some foundation training when specific areas of care will be covered.

think about

Look at the 'In Practice' on page 65. List two ways that show how you comply with each of the following aspects of standards:-

1 Health and Safety
2 Infection Control
3 Duty of Care
4 Equality and Diversity
5 Communication

How standards inform reflective practice in adult social care

Reflection or thinking about issues can be done when carrying out your job. While you are actually doing something, you may be thinking 'I can do this better' or later you may consider the reasons why you thought you could do it better and start to think of alternative ways. Get other people's perspectives as they may look at things differently to you and, together, you can come up with a solution.

The important thing is to keep asking yourself questions – but what are the questions raised when reflecting? One obvious one is 'What went well?' but there are many others.

You can record thoughts, ideas and plans in a diary, journal or learning log.

In Practice

An individual wants help to move from a bed to a chair. You risk assess the situation to ensure safety – you wash your hands; you are aware that the chair needs to be near the bed, the brakes (if any) of the bed are secured; the person needs to be moved to the edge of the bed, they may need supporting to sit up and lean forward. If their balance is poor you may reflect that two people are needed to transfer the individual safely and without hurting them. You would mention this to your team leader or manager and decide on further remedial actions.

think about ...

What questions are raised when you are thinking 'I could do better'?

Complete the other circles with some more 'evaluating' questions

What went well?

The effect of your own values, beliefs and experiences

Everyone is raised with different beliefs and values and as you grow up you notice that others' views may be different from your own, which can cause you to feel uncomfortable. You also experience different events, incidents and attitudes that will shape your behaviour and your opinions of people and situations. Sometimes these different views and attitudes lead to

We must provide the same level of care to people with different views to our own

conflicts and dilemmas but, as carers of others, it is important to accept these differences and put any prejudices aside.

You may find that your attitude towards certain values is different from that of your colleagues or those in your care. For example, you might have different ideas about motivation, conformity, cooperation, consistency, respect, fairness and creativity. This difference might be positive, as you can learn from each other.

In Practice

Suzanne is 18, a heavy smoker and drinker whose hygiene practices are poor. Her carer is a non-smoking, non-drinking older woman with high standards of cleanliness.

What attitudes could harm a relationship between Suzanne and her carer?

Miriam, a carer in a residential home, was brought up to be independent and do things for herself. She feels that her team member Mark is very fussy and helps the residents too much. She says this is spoiling them and they will expect all this help and attention from other members of staff when he is not on duty, which is unfair on others.

Suggest ways that the situation between Miriam and Mark can be a positive one.

think about

If you are part of a study group, try role playing the case study of Miriam and Mark on page 66 and allow your team mates to give positive but constructive criticism to each pair. You could re-enact the interactions with those suggestions in mind.

11.2 The importance of feedback in improving own practice

Constructive feedback

Constructive feedback is designed to support reflective practice and improve personal development and ways of working. It can be formal (for example, supervision or appraisals) or informal, after a shared task. It must not be given too long after an incident, when details may have been forgotten. It can be misinterpreted as criticism. Feedback refers to comments on our performance and is best made in a positive reflective way, for example – 'How do you think you did?' followed by some good comments and then suggestions on how you could improve.

> **Constructive feedback**
> Feedback that is intended to build on previous knowledge and used to improve performance and competence. It can be misinterpreted as criticism.
>
> **Key Term**

The importance of seeking feedback to improve practice and inform development

Some people find it difficult to receive critical constructive feedback. They may call it 'constructive criticism', although this tends to describe the feedback negatively. You may believe you have done something quite well but if your observer, a senior person, highlights errors in your performance this can be disappointing.

You need to interpret these comments constructively, that is, use them to build on your existing knowledge and skills to improve your performance and benefit those in your care. Constructive feedback raises awareness of your strengths as well as weaknesses (or areas for development) and provides a great opportunity for you to plan how to develop your strengths and minimise your weaknesses.

In Practice

During a supervision meeting, the nursing home manager comments to Mark that she has noticed he doesn't fully answer patients' queries about their medications and just says 'They will do you good'. She thinks he should give such questions more time. He is aware that his knowledge of medicines is poor.

If you were Mark, what would you do now?

The importance of seeking feedback to improve practice and inform development

It is not just your manager who can provide valuable feedback; you can also ask the individuals you care for, other professionals, relatives and teachers, assessors and your colleagues.

You are the most important motivator of your performance, the best critical assessor and the person that will offend you the least! Evaluating your own performance critically, and setting yourself targets in a self-disciplined and committed way, will reward you with the self-awareness of a knowledgeable, highly skilled professional. As you develop your skills, you will become more interested in certain areas and it is then that the 'expertise' becomes apparent.

In Practice

Elisha was a carer in the community when she became interested in why so many people were suffering infections. She was very keen on good hygiene and read a lot about infections and the immune system. She had to take more exams but progressed to become a nurse and she remained passionate about infection control. She applied and was appointed as an infection control nurse in the hospital and a few years later became the senior person responsible for public health: advising people, preventing and controlling infection in the community. By following her passions and working hard, she became a highly regarded professional, an expert in her chosen field.

What steps did Elisha take in order to continually improve in her chosen area?

By working hard in your area of interest, you can get your dream job

The importance of using feedback in your own practice

If you ignore feedback, you risk not allowing yourself to become skilful in your duties, which means you could become incompetent instead. This might lead to mistakes that could one day harm someone or result in you losing your job. As you are accountable for your actions, you must stick to agreed working practices that are linked to national standards of care.

As you have seen in the example of Elisha, acting on advice and feedback enables personal and professional progression, an increase in your level of competence and expertise and an increased self-esteem.

11.3 The personal development plan

The components of a plan

In order to develop your competencies you need to evaluate what you already know, understand and can apply in practice.

Look at the table on page 71 as an example of a carer's evaluations of her training, abilities and skill gaps.

Hypoglycaemic condition When a person feels unwell due to the lack of sugar in the circulation. People with diabetes cannot convert sugar into glucose or energy for the body and this has to be given quickly or they will collapse.

Diabetes A condition which, because of the body's failure to produce insulin (a hormone that controls sugar levels in the blood), results in the person becoming unwell. This may progress to unconsciousness unless treated.

Anaphylactic shock A severe allergic reaction that causes breathing difficulties, swelling and possibly unconsciousness.

PPE Personal and protective equipment consists of aprons, disposable gloves, hats and a uniform. They are barriers between the carer and the person (or food) intended to be protected from infection.

Invasive procedures Inserting pessaries or suppositories.

PEG feeding A specialised technique that enables medicines to be administered straight into the stomach (percutaneous endoscopic gastrostomy).

Regulation of controlled drugs Controlled drugs (CDs) are strictly regulated because they are potentially addictive and open to abuse.

Subcutaneous injections Injections inserted just under the skin with a small needle. You will require special training to administer them.

Risk assessments Steps taken to ensure that any potential hazards are assessed and the chances of the hazard occurring is reduced by taking preventive steps.

Key Terms

Training Completed/date	Knowledge and Understanding	Related practical experiences	Do I feel competent?
First Aid/ Oct 2009	How to do CPR, manage bleeding and unconsciousness. Manage choking and an allergic reaction. Recognise poor breathing patterns, signs of illness and be able to respond accordingly. Understand a **hypoglycaemic condition.**	Noticed a patient having difficulty breathing and called for assistance straight away. Managed to stop a patient from falling when he was dizzy and lie him down with legs elevated. Gave a woman suffering from **diabetes** a drink of Lucozade when she felt drowsy.	Not had to perform CPR or manage an **anaphylactic shock** or bleeding.
Infection Control/ March 2010	To wear disposable non-latex gloves and aprons when attending to patients who may be infectious and to throw away after one use. To place soiled linen in special red bags marked 'potentially infectious'.	Wearing **PPE** now without being reminded. Placing linen in the bags and cleaning up areas straight away. Wash my hands regularly between patients and apply an alcohol gel.	I do not clean and dress wounds or perform **invasive procedures.** I do not know about food safety or **PEG feeding**.
Safe Handling of Medicines/ March 2010	How to receive, store, administer and dispose of medicines. The importance of the **regulation of controlled drugs.**	Have supported the senior worker to give out medicines. I check that it is the correct person and that the person takes it and I sign the MAR sheet.	I feel competent to administer medicines but have not given any **subcutaneous injections** or administered any oxygen.
Induction Standards/ February 2010	Duty of care Safeguarding individuals in my care Effective communication Equality and diversity Health and safety	Protecting people by observing and doing **risk assessments.** Recording likes and dislikes, showing respect. Observe COSHH	I have not used the hoist and do not feel confident putting a heavy person into a bath. Not dealt with any security issues, fire hazards/evacuations.

Look at the last column in the table on page 71 about feeling competent and the dates of training. List about five learning objectives that you might plan with this carer if you were her mentor, including training needs.
Now list your own objectives and add some target dates.

A word of warning: never try to do something or perform a task for which you have not been trained!

The next step for the carer is to address the issues that would enable personal development and improve her confidence. It is useful to use the acronym SMART when setting yourself targets:

- S – Specific: ensure that your plans are specific (and simple to understand).

- M – Measurable: you can see what you have achieved against a target.

- A – Achievable: you can, with commitment, achieve your goal.

- R – Realistic: it is possible to achieve your goal.

- T – Timely: set the time that you want to achieve your plan and stick to it.

Sources of support for planning and reviewing own development

It is always a good idea to seek answers to your questions while they are fresh in your mind. Write queries down if you cannot see your manager for some time. You may find an answer by browsing the internet but remember that the internet cannot solve your practical issues and you have to be careful that you are using sources that are trustworthy. You can really only improve a performance or task through constant practice and asking for help and advice from your team leader or mentor.

You are entitled to regular supervision meetings with your line manager where you will identify issues and confirm good practice. You are also entitled to an in-depth annual appraisal. This offers you a preparation time to reflect followed by a detailed and private discussion of your progress.

Other help may come from a visiting health professional such as a nurse, a physiotherapist, occupational therapist, counsellor, pharmacist or a GP. If you ask politely, show interest and ensure that they have the time, you will get more information and perhaps the offer of work shadowing, which is a great opportunity to know how others go about their work and how you can support them and the individuals in your shared care.

You may find that updating your qualifications will help you to keep up to date with new guidelines, as legislation in the sector is changing all the time and things like emergency first aid and fire training need to be revisited often to ensure competence.

You could also ask your manager about other courses that might benefit your workplace such as dementia awareness or person-centred care although aspects of these are included in the Diploma in Health and Social Care (QCF). If you follow the apprenticeship route you will be assessed on your English, IT and numeracy skills (functional skills) as well as employment rights and responsibilities. You will also be asked to record your personal learning and thinking skills, which allows you to reflect on how you manage yourself, communicate with others, work as a team and plan ahead. You will get support from a tutor and assessor and resources that are easy to follow.

The role of others in your personal development plan

You may reflect on your own performance to identify your strong areas. However, if someone else describes a strength you have, then you should add it to your personal plan in order to develop. A second benefit of a manager recognising your abilities is that you might get support through courses, events and conferences. If your organisation supports development, it might appoint a specialist to champion its **ethos**. This is an existing member of the team so it also supports the **continuous personal development** of the staff member.

In Practice

Mark becomes interested in mental health issues. His manager has asked him to look at the conferences arranged by the Sector Skills Councils Skills for Care and Skills for Health. He finds one that appeals to him and management will pay for him to attend the conference and bring back some ideas. A short time later he starts a unit on the QCF that will help him to learn more about mental health. He feels invigorated because he is making progress in a chosen area.

Key Terms

Qualification and Credit Framework (QCF) A bank of educational courses that carry points (credits) for learning. These credits are held centrally so that learners can build on them by completing a range of short courses (at varying levels of learning) that are relevant to them. A qualification will have rules of combination to say which units of learning make up the qualification as a whole.

Ethos Believing in a particular pathway or style. An example is a home that gives a definite impression of personalised individual care or a school whose ethos is to achieve high standards and be top of the league table.

Continuous personal development (CPD) Evidence that an individual or team is continually keeping up to date, improving themselves and the organisation in which they work.

Think about your personal learning and thinking skills as they are right now. Reflect on how well you have been motivated in the past year, what topics inspire you and make you want to be more knowledgeable and skilled. In a second column jot down your aims for the next five years and compare with a friend.

Your questions answered

There are some tasks that I never get the opportunity to do but I know that doing these will help me to develop professionally. How can I make progress if I do not do things very often and these tasks remain a weakness?

It takes courage and strength to address these areas. You may want to run and hide or avoid the duty and let someone else do it. However, as time moves on and you wish to apply for another position you are expected to have the knowledge and ability to perform that duty and maybe even show others.

Difficult as it may be, the best course of action is to ask to do this duty more often, ask to be shown again or be supervised until you feel confident.

Aseptic technique A non-touch method of cleaning and dressing a wound, maintaining a sterile field – the working area that is completely free of possible harmful micro-organisms (germs) and is not contaminated (touched) by anything that is not sterile.

Key Term

In Practice

Elisha, the infection control expert, remembers being terrified of her first dressing that used an **aseptic technique**. She was being observed and feared she would contaminate the sterile field. She did make mistakes and was reluctant to perform this dressing again. Her manager, however, persuaded her to do it again and this time she was perfect and felt much better about doing it afterwards.

Can you identify your areas for development or 'fear moments' that you need to face?

How your personal development plan helps to identify ongoing improvements in knowledge and understanding

There are different ways to record your plan. You may decide to use a chart like the previous example, but your headings could be different. Below is an example that you might like to copy or adapt.

Training completed and dates	Knowledge and understanding that I need to apply	Planned development activities and dates for review
Risk assessments (October 2012)	Practise recording risk assessments	Work with team leader for three weeks, then review progress 2 December. Direct observation by assessor on 6 December. Feedback on 8 December.

You might find 'mind mapping' useful. This is similar to a spider diagram in which you record your thoughts and ideas.

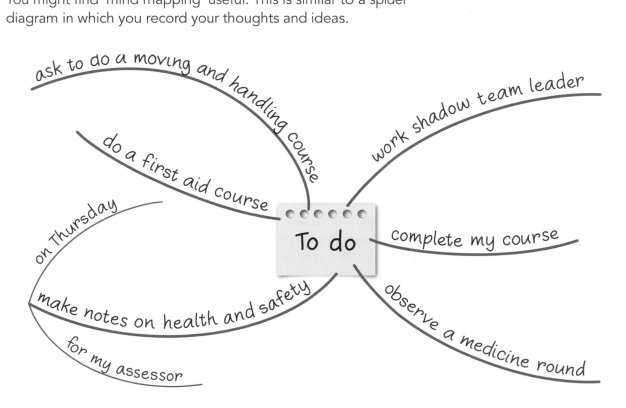

Mind maps can be a useful way of recording your ideas

Personal development – a leading charity

As a social care worker, it is essential that you keep your personal and professional development up to date. This contributes to the safeguarding of individuals and staff by ensuring that you remain up to date with the latest developments in training and legislation.

Staff need to ensure that they keep their reflective journal up to date with a variety of development methods to relate theory into practice. This will also support supervision and planning of development needs for the following year.

@work

Remember that you don't stop learning just because you complete a course. Often learning is reinforced and stronger after the course has finished. Experiences have a very strong influence on learning, which is why it is so important to reflect on these and adjust your performance to improve and develop. If you think you lack the type of experience to help you develop, then speak out and put yourself in situations that will give you those experiences.

Research is equally important and keeping up to date with the latest findings and opinions also informs good practice. For example, it is now generally accepted that it is important to focus on the positive attributes of people with disabilities and concentrate on what they can do rather than what they are unable to do.

You should make sure that you regularly re-visit the standards, look at websites and examine your own knowledge, understanding and skills base. Everyone is especially good at something and you might be able to progress in that area if you stay focused on your personal development.

Your questions answered

> **What sort of questions do I ask when I am analysing an experience?**
>
> 'What did I do well? 'What did I not do well?' 'Why was that poor?' 'How could I do it better next time?' 'What do I need to know?' and 'What do I need to ask?' 'When can I discuss it?' 'What resources can I access?' 'Who can give me specific information?' 'What timescales are realistic?'

Websites for further research

www.dh.gov.uk (information on care standards)

www.library.nhs.uk (information and research)

www.open.ac.uk (Open University resources)

www.skillsforcare.org.uk (a sector skills council for care linked to the CQC and information on social care)

www.skillsforhealth.org.uk (another sector skills council for health care)

www.nhs.uk/carers (NHS site)

https://nationalcareersservice.direct.gov.uk (linked to CQC and professional development information)

www.cqc.org.uk (Care Quality Commission)

www.hsj.co.uk (news and resources for health service workers)

Quick Quiz

1   What is the best description of reflective practice?
   a. Making lists of duties for each day
   b. Doing a task, thinking about it analytically, and planning and reviewing further ideas
   c. Arranging to work with a manager who reflects your behaviour and performance back to you
   d. Using a mirror to observe your actions

2   Reflective practice is essential for:
   a. Making shopping lists and ordering supplies
   b. Writing a care plan
   c. Doing a medicine round remembering names
   d. Continuous improvement, personally and professionally.

3   What must a healthcare professional measure performance and progress against?
   a. The care plan
   b. Timescales
   c. The national standards
   d. The job description

4   What is analysis?
   a. Interviewing people
   b. Identifying strengths and areas for improvement
   c. Asking people relevant questions in order to improve
   d. Personalised care

5   What effect do beliefs, values and experiences have?
   a. They shape our behaviour, attitudes and opinions.
   b. They make us more assertive.
   c. They make us employable.
   d. They help us to develop spiritually.

6   What can be the source of conflicts and dilemmas with others?
   a. Workers who are passive
   b. Workers who show their prejudices
   c. Workers who are senior managers
   d. Workers in the community

7   How is constructive feedback best expressed?
   a. In a strict manner
   b. Six months after an incident
   c. In a positive and well balanced way
   d. Only in formal situations

8   What is the best reason for constructive feedback?
   a. It is a requirement of Skills for Care.
   b. Without it, we might think we are better than we are.
   c. It is an effective tool to build a personal development plan.
   d. It empowers the senior manager.

9   What does a personal development plan identify?
   a. All our weaknesses
   b. Current learning and planned learning with dates and targets
   c. Tasks that are best avoided
   d. How to get a pay rise

10 How are individual issues, concerns and progress best discussed?
   a. In the corridor
   b. In a friendly resident's room with tea
   c. In a whole-team meeting
   d. In a supervision or appraisal meeting

Principles of
diversity, equality
and inclusion in
adult social care settings

This unit develops concepts of inclusion that are key to working in adult social care settings. Valuing our diverse society and working in an inclusive way enables everyone to achieve the best possible outcomes for those using services throughout the fields of health and social care. By understanding individuals and different communities in our society, you are better able to provide services that are free from discrimination, support equality and meet legal requirements.

On completion of this unit you should:

- understand the importance of diversity, equality and inclusion
- understand how to work in an inclusive way
- understand how to raise awareness of diversity, equality and inclusion

12.1 Diversity, equality and inclusion

What about influences from other countries?

With a colleague, make a list of the things in your everyday life that are influenced or come from other countries and cultures. These could be a member of your own family or a friend, music, film, travel, food, fashion or sport. List as many things as you can.

Identity

In Unit 3 (Level 2) you considered the characteristics that make up your own identity. While people share lots of characteristics, it is good to be proud of the characteristics that make you unique and special!

Some aspects of your identity that cannot be changed are:

- ethnic origin
- age.

Some characteristics are very deeply part of who you are but may be possible to change:

- gender
- religion
- nationality.

Others characteristics may change over time such as:

- abilities
- beliefs
- sexual orientation
- social class.

Diversity

Diversity Differences in culture, ability, ethnicity, gender, age, beliefs, sexual orientation and social class.

Key Term

As you learnt in Unit 3, the word 'diversity'describes the differences between individuals and groups in terms of culture, nationality, ability, ethnic origin, gender, age, religion, beliefs, sexual orientation and social class.

What do you know about individual demographic information?

Health and social care organisations are expected to collect demographic information (data such as age, location, ethnicity and disability) about their individuals.

Find out what information is collected in your organisation and how it is used.

Equality Promoting equal rights and opportunities for everyone.

Key Term

Equality

The word '**equality**' is used to support and promote the rights of individuals and groups who share characteristics. This means that people are better able or empowered to make choices and seize opportunities. When you respect people, it is more likely that you get the respect of others. As health and social care workers you are then better placed to offer services in response to the individual's need.

The legal framework

As you learnt in Unit 3, the Equality Act (2010) was brought in to consolidate the previous acts relating to protected characteristics. All service providers and employers are responsible for treating their individuals and employees fairly under the Act.

You learnt about the 'protected characteristics' in the Equality Act as it applies to individuals. To remind you, these are:

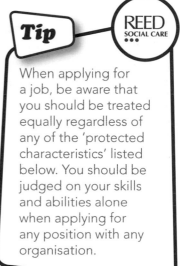

Tip

REED
SOCIAL CARE

When applying for a job, be aware that you should be treated equally regardless of any of the 'protected characteristics' listed below. You should be judged on your skills and abilities alone when applying for any position with any organisation.

- disability
- sex (gender)
- gender reassignment
- pregnancy and maternity
- race
- religion or belief
- sexual orientation
- age.

The Equality Act has a slightly different list of protected characteristics as they apply to employees. These are:

- 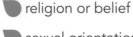 disability
- gender reassignment
- marriage or civil partnership
- pregnancy and maternity
- race
- religion or belief
- sexual orientation
- sex (gender)
- age.

The law also protects people from discrimination:
- by someone who wrongly perceives them to have one of the protected characteristics
- by being associated with someone with a protected characteristic (such as a carer, friend or relative).

Human rights

Human rights have been established as an international set of rules stating what everyone needs to live and grow; and how people should treat each other. The Universal Declaration of Human Rights was drawn up and published by the United Nations in 1948 following the Second World War. Its 30 articles support all areas of life and are included in many of the laws in this country. You will recognise many of the themes in equality and diversity and in inclusive practice within health and social care. Some of the human rights are:

- that everyone is born free and equal in dignity and rights
- the right to life, liberty and security
- the right to education
- the right to have your own thoughts, beliefs and religion
- the right to vote in elections once you reach voting age
- the right not to do forced labour or be treated as a slave.

All recruitment agencies should have a code of practice which you are able to see when working with them. If you feel that you have been discriminated against while at work via an agency, you should follow your agency's procedures to report this.

Effects of discrimination

In Unit 3 you considered the effects of discrimination in a range of situations. These included examples of:

- direct discrimination – when a person is treated worse than someone else because of a 'protected characteristic'

- indirect discrimination – when a rule or way of working has a worse impact on someone with a protected characteristic than someone without that characteristic

- institutional discrimination – when the whole organisation acts in a discriminatory way towards its individuals or customers, and/or employees because of its culture or its policies and guidelines.

It is useful to know more about the Universal Declaration of Human Rights. The Declaration and information about its history and international human rights law is published at www.un.org/en/documents/udhr

Institutional racism

The Stephen Lawrence Inquiry report (1999) described institutional racism as:

'The collective failure of an organisation to provide an appropriate and professional service to people because of their colour, culture or ethnic origin. It can be seen or detected in processes, attitudes and behaviour which amount to discrimination through unwitting prejudice, ignorance, thoughtlessness and racist stereotyping which disadvantage minority ethnic people.'

Some examples of discrimination include:

- stereotyping and labelling

- physical attacks or threats based on the person's protected characteristic

- deliberate physical and/or verbal abuse including embarrassing or derogatory remarks, jokes, name-calling and obscene gestures

- offensive communication whatever the medium (email, leaflet, poster, graffiti, imagery, internet sites)

- encouraging others to behave in a discriminatory way

Review the website of your local authority and find three or four examples of support for inclusion in society for people from minority groups (for example, groups based on race, language, age, or religion). What value do the participants place on taking part in these activities and how does the local community as a whole benefit?

How would you feel if any of these examples of discrimination were aimed at you? Putting yourself in the shoes of someone in a minority group will help you do this.

- making stereotypical assumptions about colleagues or individuals or members of the public based on their race, culture, sex, religion, belief, sexual orientation, age or disability; for example what they eat, how they pray, what they wear, and what they believe in

- patronising behaviour not used with other colleagues

- discouraging members of minority groups – either employees or members of the public – from taking up services or opportunities for advancement.

These can all lead to an individual's delay in development or care, and difficulties with self-esteem.

12.2 Working in an inclusive way

Promoting equality and supporting diversity

Inclusive practice includes:

- working in partnership and improving participation

- respecting diversity by valuing and celebrating differences between individuals and using positive images of individuals from diverse groups

- promoting rights by challenging inequality and discrimination

- promoting recovery

- understanding the person's needs and strengths and removing barriers to access or communication

- promoting ethical approaches

- promoting dignity

- person-centred care – individuals at the centre of planning and delivery of services

Inclusive practice
Working in a way that aims to include an individual or group in a positive manner by valuing their difference rather than seeing it as an issue to overcome.

Key Term

● evidence-based and values-based care

● safety and risk taking – empowering the person to make their own decisions

● supporting your own and others' personal development and learning.

In Practice

The difference between social and medical models of disability

Nick has learning difficulties and wants to live independently. His learning difficulties mean that he needs some help with shopping. Under the **social model**, Nick would be given the right support, so that he could choose to live on his own and be helped with doing his own shopping. Under the **medical model**, he would not get that choice as he would need to live in a communal home where shopping isn't offered, and his opportunities for independence are restricted.

In this example, the social model promotes Nick's equality and rights by giving him access to the services according to his needs and does not force him to have services he doesn't want.

The social model approach to supporting disability

Key Terms

Social model of disability The social model of disability relates closely to inclusive practice. It describes disability as being caused by the way society is organised, rather than by the individual's difference. When physical barriers and attitudes that restrict life choices are removed, disabled people can function in society in an equal way.

Medical model of disability The medical model looks at what is 'wrong' with the person and what needs to be 'fixed' or treated, in contrast to the social model.

Legislation and codes of practice

You learnt about the Equality Act (2010) in Unit 3.

This protects against discrimination, promotes equal opportunities and supports good relations between people with protected characteristics.

Your questions answered

> **Who are the professional regulators and what are the codes of practice/conduct that I should be aware of?**

The health and social sectors have codes of practice that everyone is expected to follow; these are drawn up and monitored by the professional regulators. These codes reflect ideas of fairness and inclusion.

Nurses and midwives are regulated by the Nursing and Midwifery Council www.nmc-uk.org

Its code of conduct (May 2008) states:

- Make the care of people your first concern, treating them as individuals and respecting their dignity.

- Work with others to protect and promote the health and well-being of those in your care, their families and carers, and the wider community.

- Provide a high standard of practice and care at all times.

- Be open and honest, act with integrity and uphold the reputation of your profession.

Social care workers, qualified social workers, and social work students on approved degree courses in England are regulated by the General Social Care Council (GSCC) www.gscc.org.uk

Interactions

In Unit 3 you learnt that you should pay attention to the following throughout your interactions at work in order to work in an inclusive way:

- listening actively

- finding out about and using your knowledge of the person's values and preferences

- reassuring the person about confidentiality and providing privacy as needed

- using appropriate language and method of communication for the person

- checking your understanding of what the person has said; and that they have understood what you have said

- being aware of how your own beliefs, culture, values and preferences may affect the way you interact with individuals and colleagues.

Consider the different needs of the following individuals when you interact with them, and the possible results of getting it wrong:

- colleagues
- adults individuals
- children and young people

Interacting at work helps improve services

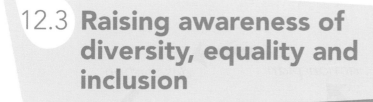

12.3 Raising awareness of diversity, equality and inclusion

Take opportunities to learn about other people's beliefs, values and traditions:

- join in cultural events with people from different backgrounds

- talk with people from other backgrounds about their beliefs and traditions.

You should speak up if others are not respecting diversity, equality, inclusion, or are acting in a discriminatory way.

Sometimes things will go wrong and you need to learn from what happened. Incidents that relate to equality and diversity need to be investigated like any other incident. Reflective practice is a useful skill to develop for studying experiences as part of a continuous learning process. It is about looking at what happened; understanding what happened and learning from it. Doing this helps you to understand the issues surrounding inclusion and to support other people's awareness and learning.

Gibb's reflective cycle

Gibb's reflective cycle is a useful model for a circular process of reflection:

- description – what happened?
- feelings – what were you feeling and thinking?
- evaluation – what was good and bad about the experience?
- analysis – what sense can you make of the situation?
- conclusion – what else could you have done?
- action plan – if it happened again, what would you do?

Taking part in and supporting reflective practice helps everyone to learn and improve.

> **66** Our first impressions are generated by our experiences and our environment… we can change our first impressions… by changing the experiences that comprise those impressions… It requires more than a simple commitment to equality. It requires that you change your life so that you are exposed to those minorities on a regular basis and become comfortable with them and familiar with the best of their culture, so that when you want to meet, hire, date, or talk with a member of a minority, you aren't betrayed by your hesitation and discomfort. **99**
>
> **Malcolm Gladwell**

Extract from *Blink: The Power of Thinking Without Thinking*, Penguin, 2006.

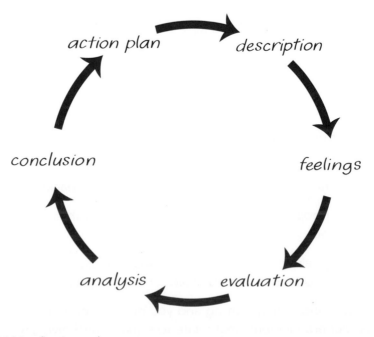

Gibb's reflective cycle

Support others to promote equality and rights

As you develop your knowledge, skills and experience in the area of equality, diversity and inclusion you should start to consider how you can best support your colleagues in health and social care by modelling excellent inclusive practice. Everyone has a responsibility to:

- understand and share information about the needs of individuals

- demonstrate ways to value differences, and recognise similarities between individuals

- highlight the benefits of cultural diversity including food, the arts and social cohesion

- set an example in appropriate use of language

- take part in and contribute to staff training activities

- follow the policies and procedures of your work setting

- demonstrate fair practice in interactions

- acknowledge other people's rights

- provide and use information on disciplinary and complaints procedures.

REED
SOCIAL CARE

Equality and diversity – a leading disability charity

The principles of equality and diversity are fundamental to our organisation, and all of our staff need to be aware of this in the way that they work. When interviewing, I look for people who display a good understanding of these principles, and who want to work in an open and inclusive way.

Challenging discrimination

Challenging discrimination must start with examining and understanding your own beliefs. You learnt that you are expected to challenge any discriminatory behaviour. Having learnt about the Equality Act and the human rights that underpin the Act, you should be able to identify any discrimination that might take place.

In Unit 3 you noted the opportunities that may be available to take part in reviewing and developing equality and diversity policies and procedures.

Human rights and the law

It is important to consider how ideas in the Equality Act (2010) and the United Nations Declaration of Human Rights, relevant British law and your organisation's policies work in practice.

As you reflect on what you have learnt about challenging discrimination, you will be able to recognise stereotypes in people's attitudes or conversation, and also in written materials.

In Unit 3 you learnt about reporting concerns and in Unit 10 you learnt about communicating concerns by whistle-blowing.

Challenging discrimination and reporting concerns can contribute to improvement and development.

What would you do?

How would you provide support for a carer who prefers to use Braille and needs information about support for their partner?

What opportunities does your organiation offer for individuals from minority ethnic groups to influence the way in which services are provided?

What would you do if an individual spoke to you or a colleague in a discriminatory way?

What do you know about your organisation's values? Look at your organisation's annual report or business plan for a statement about its values in relation human rights.

Deliberate and inadvertent discrimination

Discrimination may be deliberate (intentional or purposeful) or inadvertent (unintentional). While both are illegal, it is worth while considering how these would be dealt with in different ways.

If **deliberate discrimination** is committed by an individual as part of their work, this would be managed by grievance or disciplinary processes.

An example of **inadvertent discrimination** is where a person who does not speak English could be unaware of a service that was publicised in several languages, but not their own. The organisation itself and those commissioning services would be expected to take action to improve their understanding of the needs of the community, and promote its services to the groups that are missing out.

think about...

Look at pages 92–3 and consider the issues of older people and ageism.

Staff who develop and display the values of dignity and respect are appreciated by older people using health and social care services.

A report into NHS treatment of older people found that parts of the health service are constructed in a way that discriminates against older patients. Commissioners have tended to give services such as incontinence and falls prevention relatively low priority and funding. The report also found that older people may experience discrimination in accessing treatment for conditions such as mental health issues; and there may be under-investigation and under-treatment for conditions such as stroke, cancer and cardiology.

Using a reflective technique, consider how older people perceive and access services in your organisation or community.

www.ageuk.org.uk/health-wellbeing

Deliberate discrimination
Discrimination against a person or a group of people as a direct result of a purposeful action or omission.

Inadvertent discrimination
A situation of unequal outcomes or disadvantage for individuals or groups resulting from an action or omission that is not in itself discrimination.

Key Terms

It is important to promote health and well-being in older age

Close to home: an inquiry into older people and human rights in home care

The Equality and Human Rights Commission's inquiry into the home care of older people found that they may experience age discrimination in relation to funding and provision of home care services.

The report gave evidence of some human rights issues and made recommendations for change. Some key points from the report are summarised here.

Nearly half a million older people receive care at home, paid for in part by their local authority.

Good-quality home care helps support older people to keep their independence and live in familiar surroundings.

Although many older people receive care at home that respects and enhances their human rights, there were areas of concern in the treatment of some older people and significant shortcomings in the way that care is commissioned by local authorities. Legal safeguards are not as widely used as they should be.

Around half of the older people, friends and family members who gave evidence expressed real satisfaction with their home care. But there were concerns about human rights abuses in relation to care, which included the following:

- inadequate support for eating and drinking with an incorrect belief that health and safety rules prevent care workers preparing hot meals

- physical abuse, such as rough handling or physical force

- tasks in the care package not being carried out due to lack of time, resulting in neglect

- financial abuse, for example money being stolen

- lack of respect for privacy and dignity when carrying out intimate tasks

- talking over or patronising older people

- social isolation and loneliness because of a lack of support to take part in community life

- insufficient choice for older people about how and when their home care is delivered.

The impact of these abuses on older people can be depressing and stressful. Some instances of a lack of dignity could easily be put right.

The report concluded that many of the practices reported were due to systemic problems and a failure to apply a human rights approach to home care provision, rather than the fault of individual care workers.

www.equalityhumanrights.com/homecareinquiry

Empowering people with dementia

The Charter of Rights for People with Dementia and their Carers in Scotland decribes the principal rights to which people with dementia should be entitled.

People with dementia and their carers deserve the same human rights as everyone else. Unfortunately, in addition to the impact of the illness, people with dementia may experience cultural, social and economic barriers to these rights. People with dementia have the right to:

- access appropriate care and encouragement in terms of protection and rehabilitation

- help to achieve and maintain independence, ability, inclusion and participation in all aspects of life

- access opportunities for education and learning

- access social and legal services to maintain their care, protection from harm and autonomy to make choices

- health and social care services that are provided by staff and professionals with appropriate training that ensures services of the highest quality.

www.dementiarights.org

Websites for further reading and research

www.dementiarights.org (Dementia support)

www.gscc.org.uk (The General Social Care Council)

www.skillsforcareanddevelopment.org.uk (Sector Skills Council for Care and Development)

www.skillsforhealth.org.uk (Skills for Health)

Quick Quiz

1   Which of the following people is likely to be affected by homophobic behaviour?
   a. A transgender person
   b. A gay or lesbian person
   c. A bisexual person
   d. All of the above

2   Sexual orientation describes which of the following?
   a. Attraction to the opposite sex and the same sex
   b. Attraction to neither sex
   c. Attraction to the same sex only
   d. All of the above

3   Which of these aspects of a person's life may not be affected by discrimination?
   a. Freedom to attend your church
   b. Opportunities in education
   c. Getting a day off to go to a football match
   d. Having a choice of food as a resident in a care home that conforms to your religious beliefs

4   Which of these criteria do not describe someone's religious or philosophical beliefs?
   a. Collective worship
   b. An allergy
   c. A clear belief system
   d. A profound belief affecting the person's way of life

5   Which of these is a possible consequence of not complying with legislation and codes of practice relating to diversity, equality, inclusion and discrimination?
   a. Individuals feeling involved in their care
   b. Individuals missing out on available services
   c. Carers' needs being met
   d. All employees getting fair opportunities for promotion

6   Which of the following is not an example of human rights failures in the report 'Close to home: an inquiry into older people and human rights in home care'?
   a. Physical abuse, such as rough handling or physical force
   b. Financial abuse, for example money being stolen
   c. Lack of respect for privacy and dignity when carrying out intimate tasks
   d. Talking to older people

7   Which of the following activities does not specifically support diversity?
   a. Having a party
   b. Valuing differences between individuals
   c. Using positive images of individuals from diverse groups
   d. Celebrating differences

8   Which of these actions should you take if you think that your manager is discriminating against an individual?
   a. Report it to your chief executive.
   b. Reflect on it; check your understanding with a senior colleague and then make arrangements to ask your manager about what happened.
   c. Write a letter to the Caldicott Guardian.
   d. Phone a local radio phone-in show.

9   Which of these is subject to the Equality Act?
   a. Equal prices in every shop in town
   b. Equal number of rooms on every floor of a residential home
   c. Equal waiting times for a service for everyone referred to it
   d. Equal number of leaflets printed in every language

10 Which of these is not a human right?
   a. Equal pay
   b. Security
   c. Respect
   d. Medical care

Principles for
implementing duty
of care in health, social care
or children's and young
people's settings

The concept of owing a duty of care is relevant for you and all health and social care workers. It is the basis of good, safe practice and will guide you in your day-to-day work.

People may have a duty of care if their action or inaction is likely to cause harm to another person. Duty of care involves thinking about the consequences of your actions (or inaction) on other people. It relates to many aspects of life and is of particular significance in the health and social care sector.

On completion of this unit you should:

- understand how duty of care contributes to safe practice
- know how to address conflicts or dilemmas that may arise between an individual's rights and the duty of care
- know how to respond to complaints

13.1 How duty of care contributes to safe practice

Duty of care for health and social care workers

At work, duty of care means you are accountable for your action or inaction (omission). You must be able to justify your actions and show that you have taken reasonable care. You must work safely and carry out your duties competently, doing what you are employed to do. You will need to undertake training and updates in order to maintain your competence and skills

In your workplace, there will be policies and agreed **standard procedures** that must be followed by all staff. There may also be a **code of practice** that describes the required standard of behaviour and provides guidance on ways of working. It is essential that you maintain confidentiality and keep accurate health and social care records. You must also be aware of professional boundaries and ensure that you do not favour one individual to the disadvantage of another. You should always monitor your own behaviour and change it if you realise it is not appropriate. If you are not sure about any aspect of your work, or if you have concerns, then you must speak up straightaway.

This is your duty of care and it will help to protect both you and individuals using the care service. It is not something extra: it is central to all that you do at work.

did you know?

Duty of care is relevant to many aspects of day-to-day life?

Work within the boundaries of your job role

- Working within the boundaries of your job role
- What you are doing and why; be prepared to explain your reasons
- Being assertive and saying what you can and cannot do and encouraging other staff to do this
- How you delegate work to others (if this is part of your role)
- How you access training and updates
- How you deal with personal data and confidential information
- Who can help you if you need advice

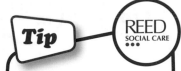

Tip

You should ensure that you remember examples of when you have done these things in the workplace. Referring to real examples in interview will add strength to your interview answers.

Your questions answered

Do I have a duty of care when I delegate work to others?

When delegating work to other members of staff, you must ensure the following:

 Is it part of their work role?

 Is it consistent with workplace policies and procedures?

 Have they have been given appropriate training and supervision and therefore have the ability to perform the delegated duties?

If this is the case and they accept the task, then they are responsible for what they do.

Note: You are responsible for the appropriateness of the delegation.

At work you have a duty of care to users of your care service, your colleagues, employer and the public. Your colleagues and employer also have a duty of care to you.

How duty of care contributes to the safeguarding and protection of individuals

Tip

REED
SOCIAL CARE
●●●

Safeguarding is high in the minds of every employer in the social care sector. You should fully understand this topic and legislation surrounding it prior to interview.

Many individuals who receive a care service are potentially more at risk of harm, abuse, intimidation and humiliation than others are. Safeguarding is discussed in detail in Unit 4 but it is important to understand that your duty of care is part of the safeguarding process.

Using equipment and resources correctly, ensuring privacy or simply the way you talk to an individual, are all ways in which you contribute to the safety and well-being of individuals receiving care services. There are different ways of working in different places, but a responsible, caring and compassionate approach is relevant to all health and social care workers and all situations.

In Practice

Jim, a care worker, was helping Bill to move from his chair. He decided to use a new piece of equipment (a standing aid) which required the individual to be able to bear weight. Jim had recently been trained on this new equipment and he liked it. He didn't feel it was necessary to check Bill's care plan and so he was not aware that this type of standing aid was not suitable for Bill. As Jim used the equipment, Bill felt afraid, he panicked and slipped.

- If a care worker does something with an individual that is not consistent with the care outlined in their plan, then consequences can be very serious for both the worker and the individual.

- If the care delivered falls below the necessary standard, this can be described as a breach in the duty of care.

- If duty of care is breached due to actions or omissions, then an individual can bring a legal case for negligence.

 Would Jim be able to justify his actions and show that he took reasonable care ?

Accidents can happen; however, this was a foreseeable and unnecessary risk. Jim did not check the plan of care, and this individual was not able to use this type of standing aid. Jim did not safeguard the interests of Bill and so failed to meet his duty of care.

13.2 Individual rights and duty of care: managing conflicts and dilemmas

People have the right to live their life the way that they want to as long as they are acting within the law and not harming others. Many people who are receiving care can experience a loss of individual rights and autonomy. Often, care workers, in their willingness to assist and protect, overlook the importance of the individual's choice and personal responsibility. This can result in conflict and dilemmas, as some individuals may wish to participate in what may be unsafe behaviours. For example, they may stay out without permission, go somewhere without telling anyone, abuse drugs or alcohol or become involved in vandalism. Equally, they might also want to do things that they see other people doing, such as having sexual relationships. It is important to recognise that individuals receiving care services should be able express their wishes and opinions, while at the same time feeling safe and secure and having a sense of belonging.

Remember, duty of care requires the health and social care worker to support the individual to understand the choices they have and to exercise their individual rights. It is not your role to control an individual or to remove these rights to make choices. An important way to achieve a more balanced approach is through providing information, communicating effectively and making the relationship between the worker and the individual more equal.

If you broke a glass at home, how would you dispose of it? Would you just throw it straight into the bin?

Is it acceptable to park a car across the pavement and force people with prams or wheelchair users on to a busy road?

If you noticed that a large tree from your garden was about to fall into your neighbour's garden would you be concerned?

Managing risk and duty of care

Care workers may sometimes feel worried about individuals undertaking certain activities because of the risk of harm and the possibility that the worker may be seen as negligent and blamed if things go wrong. Although duty of care involves managing risks, it does not mean that it is possible or desirable to remove all risk.

Due to limited time and resources, sometimes you may feel under pressure and unable to deliver the care that is needed, or you

Duty of care involves managing risk not removing all risk

did you know?

Duty of care involves thinking about the consequences of actions or inactions and taking steps to avoid foreseeable harm.

find out!

Are you fully updated regarding your organisation's guidelines and policies?

Your duty of care requires staff to carry out procedures and day-to-day work with reasonable skill and care – this means that you must be up to date.

think about...

Brad lives in a flat with a shared entrance hall. There is a front door and a fire exit at the back. Brad always chains his bicycle to a pipe next to the fire exit obstructing this exit. Does Brad have a duty of care to the others who live in his block of flats?

may observe some bad practice. Your duty of care means that you are required to report it and follow your local system for raising concerns. If you make a mistake, again your duty of care requires you to report what has happened and be open and honest.

Principles for implementing duty of care

- Promote independence.
- Act in the best interests of the individual.
- Avoid harm.
- Be truthful and honest.

By applying these established principles, you will be working safely and protecting both individuals you provide a care service to and yourself.

What would you do?

You are a key worker for Deanna (19). She wants to have a sexual relationship with Zac (31). You are concerned about this as Deana has a mild learning disability and has only recently met Zac.

- Listen and talk to Deanna.
- Establish and maintain trust and confidence.
- Follow workplace policies and procedures guidelines, and the workplace code of practice.
- Assess risks.
- Plan.
- Work in partnership.
- Access additional support.
- Keep good health and social care records.
- Raise concerns if necessary.

Care services should have agreed safe ways of working, policies and protocols in order to reduce of the risk of harm. If these are followed, staff are protected and individuals can be empowered. Staff can feel confident that they are fulfilling their duty of care to the individuals – correctly balancing health and safety issues with individual rights and choices.

Where to get additional support

You are not expected to make difficult decisions at work alone and there are many sources of support available to you. A complex situation may be new to you, but your manager may have experience of similar circumstances. There are also other specialist health and social care workers who can advise on specific issues.

Further support can be obtained from outside your workplace. Many organisations that have a responsibility to promote the safety and well-being of individuals receiving care also support the workers who deliver this service.

Tip

Regardless of whether you start a permanent or temporary position, you should familiarise yourself with the policies of the organisation where you work.

Where can I get support?	
Line manager	Day-to-day guidance, agreed ways of working
Tutors and trainers	Up-to-date information on latest developments
The wider health and social care team	E.g., physiotherapists, specialist nurses – detailed knowledge of a specialist area
Schools/colleges	May be able to offer guidance regarding a specific issue
Counselling services	An individual can talk through an issue with a counsellor
Mediation	Neutral person/service may intervene to help resolve difficulties
Advocacy services	Ensure that individuals wishes are expressed and rights protected

Additional support – a UK Care Home Group

Nobody who works for us is expected to manage everything on their own. Support is always available if required, and it's better to ask for help than try to manage something if you are unsure. Trying to cope with something you are not equipped to deal with can have serious consequences – from day one here, if you need help, ask!

@work

13.3 Responding to complaints

A complaint can be described as an expression of dissatisfaction or concern. It can be given verbally or in writing.

Individuals have the right to complain about the care that they receive or if they feel it has not met the required standard.

Sometimes individuals are reluctant to complain because they fear that this could make matters worse.

It is important that people know how to make complaints and how to give feedback regarding a care service. They must also be assured that all complaints will be dealt with sensitively and positively. This approach will create openness, as people can raise concerns and staff will have an opportunity to respond and improve practice if necessary. A clear and straightforward complaints procedure will protect the rights of individuals.

- Listen to what the person is saying, and don't interrupt. If they are angry or upset, show them that you are interested and concerned.

'Everyone else likes the food!'

- Reassure the person that you will do something and that you are glad that they have told you that they are unhappy.

- Don't get angry or defensive – this could inflame the situation and make things worse.

- Do not make excuses or blame other staff.

- Provide information and advice on procedures for complaining.

- Explain to the person what you are going to do and then do it.

- Report to your manager.

- Learn from what has happened and reflect on complaints to improve your practice

Agreed procedures for handling complaints

All complaints should be taken seriously. If you receive a verbal complaint, it is good practice to respond immediately. If you cannot do this, refer the matter to your manager/supervisor straight away. It may be possible to resolve the situation at this stage; if not, the complainant will need to put their concerns in writing. Whatever outcome at this stage, record details of the complaint.

If a complaint is being made on behalf of an individual, it is necessary to confirm that they have consented to this.

Written complaints must be acknowledged within a short timescale, usually two to three days. It is important to find out what went wrong and a manager will conduct an investigation. There will be a timescale in which the person who is making the complaint receives a response. A meeting between the complainant and the investigating manager may be convened at an appropriate time. The next phase is all about putting things right. When complaints are handled in this way, it is referred to as local resolution.

If the complainant is not satisfied with the response, they can take the complaint to the Local Government Ombudsman. This is an independent authority that investigates complaints and shares the findings to improve practice.

Tip

Recruitment agencies will have a complaints policy which you should familiarise yourself with when working in a temporary position. Your agency will need to be informed of any issues or complaints while you are working for them.

find out!

It is important that you know how individuals can make complaints or raise concerns in your workplace.

- What is the complaints procedure in your workplace?
- Do people have the opportunity to provide general feedback, without wishing to make a particular complaint?

Offering comments cards or some other way of obtaining general feedback from individuals can be helpful and can sometimes prevent the need to complain.

Complaints Policy and Form

A complaints policy could include:

- An introduction to state that your advocacy scheme aims to provide high quality services, but would like people you support and external agencies to let you know whether anything can be improved.
- The procedure for people you support or external agencies to make a complaint or raise a concern.
- How long it will take for the advocacy scheme to respond.
- How the advocacy scheme will respond.
- The procedure that individuals should follow if they are not satisfied with the advocacy scheme's initial response – e.g. a letter to the Chairperson.
- The procedure if person is still not satisfied – e.g. will it be taken to a management committee meeting?
- Also invite positive feedback.
- What support will people you support receive when they plan to make a complaint? Do you have a reciprocal agreement with another advocacy scheme?

Complaints Form

Date of complaint	
Nature of complaint	
Key issues	
Action points as a result of the complaint	
Date Trustees informed, and their comments	
Date complaint resolved	
Outstanding action points	

Organisational complaints policy

Quick Quiz

1. Which of the following helps you to fulfil your duty of care?
   a. Understanding your work role
   b. Following the workplace code of practice, policies and procedures
   c. Keeping up to date with knowledge and skills
   d. All of the above

2. A new piece of moving and handling equipment is available in your workplace. What do you do?
   a. Have a play with it until you work out how to use it.
   b. Attend the training session arranged by your manager.
   c. Use it straightaway with a client because you have seen one before.
   d. Lock it away in the store cupboard and don't go near it.

3. At work, you have a duty of care to:
   a. colleagues
   b. carers and relatives
   c. the public
   d. all of the above.

4. Training and update information is:
   a. for new staff only
   b. only for experienced staff
   c. part of your duty of care
   d. helpful but not essential.

5. If duty of care is breached due to actions or inaction, which of the following could happen?
   a. An individual is harmed.
   b. A legal case for negligence is brought.
   c. The reputation of the organisation is badly affected.
   d. All of the above

6. If a relative wants to make a complaint, what do you do?
   a. Listen to their concerns and inform them of the complaints procedure.
   b. Tell them to speak to the setting's manager.
   c. Say it is not your fault.
   d. Explain that the individual can be difficult.

7. Complaints must be responded to:
   a. within an agreed short timescale stated in the workplace policy
   b. at a convenient time for the workers
   c. only once all the evidence has been collected
   d. at the manager's discretion.

8. Which of the following is not an appropriate person or group to help you if you need guidance when facing a conflict over rights and choices at work?
   a. Your partner
   b. Your manager
   c. Advocacy services
   d. Mediation services

9. If a health and social care worker is not able to explain what they have done and show that they have taken reasonable care, this is:
   a. a breach of the Equality Act
   b. a breach of duty of care
   c. a breach of safeguarding
   d. a breach of the Data Protection Act.

10. Duty of care is:
    a. an advanced experience
    b. an additional module in your qualification
    c. the foundation of good practice
    d. only relevant to new staff.

Understand
person-centred approaches in
adult social care settings

This unit draws together themes from many other modules, including the ideas of communication, equality, safety, duty of care, personal development and the role of the health and social care worker. The idea and process of person-centred care is central to providing excellent health and social care. This unit examines person-centred values, the reasons why these influence all aspects of care, and some of the theories that have guided society's understanding of human needs, motivation and fulfilment. The idea of person-centred support as a fundamental principle of adult social care is explored in the context of individuals with a variety of conditions and needs.

On completion of this unit you should:

- understand person-centred approaches in adult social care

- understand how to implement a person-centred approach in an adult social care setting

- understand the importance of establishing consent when providing care or support

- understand how to implement and promote active participation

- understand how to support an individual's right to make choices

- understand how to promote an individual's well-being

- understand the role of risk assessment in enabling a person-centred approach

You or those close to you may have received services in the past – perhaps in a health and social care setting, or from other services such as education, the police, a job centre, a housing association etc. Reflect on the person centred values you experienced – what was good and what could have been improved upon? What could you learn from your experience to improve your understanding of the value of a person centred approach?

14.1 Person-centred approaches in adult social care

Unit 7 (Level 2) recognised that the individual exists within a network of family, friends and the wider community, rather like your Facebook network. The notion of 'systems thinking' involves thinking of all parts in relation to the whole, because all parts function together and respond to each other. By thinking about the dynamic (constantly changing) nature of a person in relationship to their community and the wider environment, you can consider the consequences of a change in one part of the system on the rest of it. So, for example, if a person becomes ill, this will have consequences for their family, friends, work colleagues and the wider community (for example, the health and social care services).

Person-centred values

As you learnt in Unit 7, at the core of person-centred care – designing it, planning it, providing it, evaluating it and making changes in response to that evaluation – are a set of principles. As you reflect on the units you have completed so far, these topics will be familiar:

- individuality – the person's uniqueness (Unit 7)

- rights – the person's human rights and their rights under British law and within our policies and procedures (Unit 12)

- choice – in what care our individuals have, and how they have it (Unit 7)

- privacy – to have conversations, care and treatment away from others (Unit 7)

- independence – to live life without interference (Unit 7)

- **dignity** and respect – treating people with full consideration of their human rights (Unit 12)

- partnership – to plan and agree care as an equal partner (Unit 12)

Dignity Closely related to human rights, dignity is about the idea of respect and status and is at the core of person-centred values.

Key Term

Assessing care needs

A person-centred approach to care includes assessing the person's needs, active communication, planning and reviewing. In doing this, you pay attention to the person's rights for independence, choice and to be included and valued.

14.2 Implementing person-centred approaches

Unit 7 showed that person-centred care planning is expected throughout all aspects of adult and social care. People who may have vulnerabilities, such as learning difficulties, physical disabilities and mental health issues, deserve a knowledgeable and skilled person-centred approach to their assessment, planning and care giving. This is underpinned by the key principles of:

- respecting the person's rights and their unique circumstances

- maintaining and supporting independence as much as possible

- enabling positive decisions and healthy choices by providing reliable and relevant information

- inclusion, reflecting the person's individuality, culture, values and diversity.

Person-centred approaches according to level of need

The health and social care system should organise care provision in a way that meets the different levels of need in that specific community or population. People with long-term conditions usually want and are often able to 'self-manage' their condition with minimal input from professionals. Person-centred care in this context includes providing inclusive information.

Person-centred care planning

Person-centred thinking skills Considering the person as a whole, and as part of their own network.

Total communication Including meeting the person's communication needs and active listening.

Essential lifestyle planning How their lifestyle contributes to their well-being.

Person-centred reviews Evaluating the person's care while paying attention to other changes going on around them.

Key Terms

Tip

Employers will ask for examples of where you have implemented a person-centred approach in the past. Consider making a note of examples of where you have done this, which you canuse at interview.

If a person has more acute health and social care needs, in the Kaiser system (see below) the person would be in the 'disease management' group, requiring flexible, person-centred care in response to their health and social care needs.

Using a model such as the Kaiser triangle model, a person-centred approach for the individual's needs is combined with society's need for health promotion, prevention and effective use of tax-payers' money for those needing input to their health and social care needs. This model is particularly relevant for those with long-term conditions; for example many people with diabetes, respiratory conditions, cardiovascular conditions, neuromuscular and musculoskeletal conditions and cancer may require different levels of health and social care support over potentially long periods.

Case management for people with highly complex needs

Disease management for patients with high risk

Supported self care for 70% – 80% of people with long-term conditions

Population-wide prevention

The Kaiser triangle model shows different levels of care

Person-centred support

Places for People have set up a project group to look at how best to develop personalised services and to meet the personalisation agenda. This group has gathered specific examples of good practice from our schemes and is using this information to challenge all our staff to review the way that they work with customers. Training for staff has been developed to ensure that they are able to really understand what is important for the individual and to think about innovative ways of meeting these needs. Our support planning process looks at the outcomes that the customers want – so we are not looking at what support people 'need' but what they really want to achieve in their lives. This may seem a simple change to make but has made a significant difference to the support that we offer and the way that our staff work with customers.

@work

Planning care

The care plan will include a record of the person's assessed needs and preferences throughout their care, treatment and support. If the person feels ownership of their care plan and the person-centred decision making that created it; they should feel confident in the care delivery. Their requirements, preferences and choices come together to reflect a **holistic** approach (the person as a whole, including their range of needs, their background, family and place in the community).

Whatever format is used, the person's care plan documents the assessment, planning, detail of the care given and evaluating the success in meeting the person's care needs. Remember that in the care process, if something has not been written down, it might as well have not happened. All members of the multi-disciplinary team need to have access to and use of the care documentation to reduce errors and duplication. As discussed in Unit 7, if the individual holds their own care plan this demonstrates a genuine approach to ownership and person-centred care.

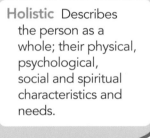

Holistic Describes the person as a whole; their physical, psychological, social and spiritual characteristics and needs.

Key Term

Working in a person-centred way

Working towards person-centred care means:

- involving the person in planning and providing their own care
- finding out about the person as an individual, their history and preferences, in a non-judgemental way
- involving the entire multi-disciplinary team as well as the person's family members, and advocates
- working with the person's values and beliefs; their strengths and potential
- ensuring equality and inclusive practice throughout
- creating a therapeutic environment (one that supports positive care giving)
- working towards a feeling of well-being by supporting the person's physical and emotional needs
- being focused on positive outcomes and the person's satisfaction with their care
- adapting and modifying the interventions and approach to reflect changes in the person's physical condition, treatment needs, preferences or circumstances.

Handling complex or sensitive situations

Sooner or later you are sure to come across challenging situations in a range of health and social care situations. You should be sure that you have the support you need from more senior colleagues as you develop your knowledge, skills and experience in these areas – do not think that you have to cope by yourself.

Situations that may be distressing or traumatic include:

- bereavement
- threatening, frightening or violent behaviour
- incidents that are likely to have serious implications
- a sudden worsening of the person's condition
- incidents that are likely to have personal consequences, such as those involving confidential information
- interactions involving complex communication or special cognitive needs, for instance individuals with communication or learning difficulties.

Your questions answered

> **Tell me more about Life Story work**

You learnt a little about Life Story work in Unit 7. It is a process of 'getting to know' a person. It aims to improve the quality of life and well-being of the person by enabling them to document and share their story in a way that suits them. It includes looking back and remembering the past and understanding the person's current hopes and dreams, such as spending time with their family. Life Story work is usually one-to-one and can take many forms – a book; a sheet of paper, a computer file, a selection of photographs, a recording of stories and sounds. Here are a few questions to get started:

- Where did you grow up?
- What did your parents do for a living?
- Where did you go to school?
- Where did you go on holiday or for a day out?
- Did you have any pets?
- What is your idea of a treat?
- Tell me about someone who you really admire.
- What makes you laugh?
- Tell me about something in your life that you are really proud of.

www.lifestorynetwork.org.uk

14.3 Establishing consent when providing care or support

Capacity to express consent

Some individuals may not have the knowledge and understanding to give valid consent. This is known as lacking 'capacity'. Factors that may affect the person's capacity are:

- mental impairment
- physical illness
- learning difficulties
- language barriers.

Do not assume that these factors automatically mean that an individual does not have capacity. They may be able to make relevant choices, decisions and give consent.

You might try:

- working sensitively with individuals by giving time and space for questions and reflection
- adapting working approaches such as providing access to information in a way that the person finds helpful and supporting them in evaluating risks
- using physical or communication aids, for example use of appropriate language and translation,

Of course, you should also seek help where necessary.

Safeguarding vulnerable adults is covered in Unit 4.

Your questions answered

> **What is meant by 'lacking capacity'?**
>
> The Mental Capacity Act (2005) Code of Practice (see www.direct.gov.uk and search for 'mental capacity act') gives guidance to people working with adults who may lack capacity to make certain decisions.
>
> Lacking capacity means lacking ability to make a decision or take an action at the time the decision or action is needed. This could be the result of impairment or disturbance. In assessing capacity, an assessment is made of
>
> - the person's general understanding of what decision is being made
> - the person's understanding of the likely consequences of making or not making the decision
> - whether the person is able to understand, retain, balance and use the relevant information
> - whether the person can communicate the decision.

Establishing consent

Establishing consent is the process of reaching an informed agreement to an action or decision with individuals. To do this you need to ensure that the individual has access to the appropriate information. Your communication skills – verbal, non-verbal and written – and active listening allow you to make a judgement about whether the person has reached a valid decision to consent. The importance of consultation and inclusive communication is clear in order to reach 'informed consent' by:

- respecting the person's choices
- listening and responding to the individual's questions and concerns

- responding appropriately

- working to resolve any conflicts if consent cannot be established

- seeking extra support and advice where necessary.

For some treatments and interventions, a formal consent document will be used; for example, for a surgical procedure, having an anaesthetic, taking part in research or making financial arrangements. Many day-to-day interventions rely on informal, verbal consent such as, 'I'm going to [do this], is that OK?' Sometimes implied consent may exist, for example if the person chooses to take their medication or holds their arm out to give a blood sample, but you need to ensure that the reason for the treatment has been explained.

14.4 Active participation in care

Active participation

Physical disability may be a barrier to active participation

Active participation means empowering a person to take part in the activities and relationships of everyday life as independently as possible. The individual should be an active partner in their own care or support, rather than a passive recipient. Information and education can support and empower a person to participate in their own care. By actively managing their own condition, such as diabetes or asthma, a person is likely to take responsibility and benefit from improved outcomes. Feelings of well-being result from a person's increased independence and autonomy.

Possible barriers to active participation include:

- learning difficulties

- physical disability

- language barriers.

But there are ways to reduce barriers to active participation, including the use of physical, communication or visual aids. In social care, personal budgets (see Unit 7) are a good example of how an individual's own choices and priorities can be achieved, contributing to their overall well-being.

Shared decision making

Shared decision making describes an ideal position between the traditional paternalistic approach and that of informed choice, where the patient or individual expects or needs the expertise of the professional.

The shared decision-making approach is based on the understanding that:

- people are more motivated to take advice and follow treatment plans when they understand the reasons and thinking behind their care, so treatment is more successful

- when given the right support and information, patients usually choose more cost-effective options.

The Health Foundation describes the idea of shared decision making as a process in which patients are encouraged to participate in selecting appropriate treatments or management options.

Not being properly told about their illness and the options for treatment is the most common cause of patient dissatisfaction. Most patients nowadays want more information and a greater say in decisions about how they will be treated.

While the concept of shared decision making is primarily about the clinician/patient relationship, the idea translates well to all interactions between health and social care professionals and individuals. See the feature on shared decision making on p116.

find out!

Review the website of your local authority and find three or four examples of support to enable active participation in society for people with learning difficulties, physical disabilities and language barriers. What value do the participants place on taking part in these activities and how does the local community as a whole benefit?

Shared decision making

In shared decision making (SDM), patients are involved as active partners with the clinician in clarifying acceptable medical options and choosing a preferred course of clinical care. Choosing an appropriate treatment with full patient involvement can be a complex process. It involves a number of steps.

- Recognise and clarify the problem.

- Identify potential solutions.

- Discuss options and uncertainties.

- Provide information about the potential benefits, harm and uncertainties for each option.

- Check understanding and uncertainties.

- Agree a course of action.

- Implement the chosen treatment.

- Arrange follow up.

- Evaluate the outcome.

Shared decision making is appropriate in any situation when there is more than one reasonable course of action, and no particular option is self-evidently best for everyone. This situation is very common because there are often many different ways to treat a health problem, each of which may lead to a different set of outcomes. These are known as 'preference-sensitive' decisions. In these cases ,the patient's attitude to the likely benefits and risks should be a key factor in the decision making. The principles of shared decision making ought to be observed whenever clinicians have to obtain informed consent or communicate risks.

Shared decision making relies on two sources of expertise:

- the health professional is an expert on the effectiveness, probable benefits and potential harms of treatment options

- the patient is an expert on themselves, their social circumstances, attitude to illness and risk, values and preferences.

www.health.org.uk

Implementing and promoting active participation

In any health and social care setting, you should always find ways to encourage individuals to take the lead in their care, in whatever way feels right for them. You can do this by paying attention to the person at the centre of their family and community, and understanding their holistic (physical, emotional and spiritual) needs. Sometimes you need to find ways to support individuals in changing their behaviours to adopt a healthy lifestyle; learning about theories of motivation can help in finding approaches that suit the individual.

Your questions answered

What is motivation?

Motivation is what drives a person's goal-orientated behaviour. It is what causes people to do something, whether it is a short- or long-term action. Motivational forces may be:

- biological
- social
- emotional
- cognitive (the mental processes of perception, memory, judgement and reasoning).

Several different theories explain motivation.

- Instinct theory – based on evolutionary programmed or inherent behaviour
- Incentive theory – based on external rewards such as one's salary

- Drive theory – based on the preference to reduce internal tensions caused by unmet, usually biological, needs
- Arousal theory – based on the need to increase or reduce arousal by balancing activity and rest; entertainment and boredom
- Humanistic theory – based on the idea that people have strong cognitive reasons to take actions (this is described in Maslow's hierarchy of needs in Unit 7).

In practice it is possible to motivate people by using incentives, and by highlighting the advantages and benefits of active participation in care and making healthy choices.

14.5 The individual's right to make choices

Choice and empowerment

In order to support an individual's empowerment, you should pay attention to:

- independence and autonomy of individuals

- impartiality

- your own attitudes, values and beliefs

- not allowing your own personal values to influence an individual's decision making.

Human rights

The Universal Declaration of Human Rights was considered in Unit 12. Human rights are established in the law; many human rights are expressed in the Equality Act, which specifically makes it illegal to discriminate against people on the basis of characteristics such as race, sex, age, sexual orientation and disability.

Support the individual's right to make choices

Developing respectful relationships relies on non-judgemental communication, inclusive information and respecting an individual's choices.

Health and social care services use agreed risk assessment processes to support individuals in making health and lifestyle choices and decisions about treatment or care. This helps to ensure that the person is aware of actual or potential harmful effects arising from their choices, such as increased vulnerability, impact on treatment, recovery or longer-term outcomes.

Health and social care support staff have a role in empowering and supporting individuals to question or challenge decisions about them that are made by others; you may need to spend some time with the person while they consider such information. In your role you may find yourself advocating for the person: supporting their choices and speaking up for them if there is discriminatory practice. This demands confidence and assertiveness, knowledge of relevant legislation and agreed ways of working. You will need to work with more experienced colleagues to develop these skills, and seek support when necessary.

> **Tip**
> **REED SOCIAL CARE**
>
> Always remember that you have the right to make choices about your career. Interviewing for a position does not mean that you have to take the position if offered – as it may not be right for you. Make sure that you make the right choices for you, as your career will take up a large part of your life.

14.6 Promoting the individual's well-being

Health and social care services are about creating, promoting and supporting the **well-being** of people. Different services support well-being for different groups in the population; for those people with long-term health conditions and social care needs, and for those with acute physical and mental health needs and short-term social care support.

While supporting a person's expressed primary need, it is important to pay attention to other needs. For example, a person may have an acute or long-term health need. To provide person-centred care, it is also necessary to consider their mental health needs, such as depression, or any social care needs associated with their main problem, or existing alongside it. By doing this, you are offering the best chance of promoting the person's overall well-being.

> **Well-being** Factors such as biological, health, spiritual, emotional, cultural, religious, social satisfaction come together to create a person's well-being.
>
> **Key Term**

Underpinning theories

You have already briefly looked at some theories of motivation. You will now consider two of the models that explain the underlying structures of human needs and preferences. By learning a little about these ideas, you can add some structure to your own understanding and practice. You will notice that both these models describe an 'actualising' preference. Maslow's model applies to humans, while Rogers believed that all life forms try to make the best of their existence – have you noticed how determined some weeds can be to grow in your garden?

Abraham Maslow

As you learnt in Unit 7, Maslow's model explains why a person must have their most basic needs met before addressing their higher needs. The hierarchy describes the fact that, in order for people to reach their maximum potential, their basic physical and psychological needs must first be met. These build upon each other, from the base of the pyramid, starting with physiological needs (the most basic needs that are vital to survival). At the top of the pyramid is Maslow's idea of 'self-actualisation' (self-awareness and concern with personal growth and fulfilment).

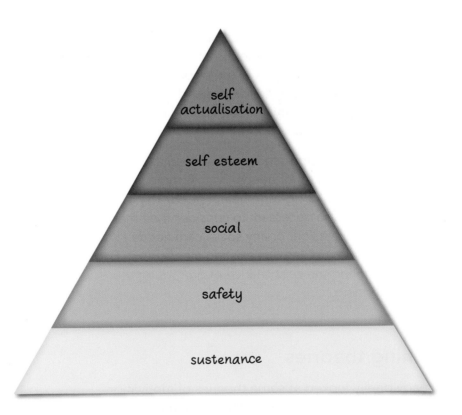

Maslow's hierarchy of needs

Carl Rogers

Unit 7 also considered Carl Rogers' theory, which uses the idea of the 'actualising tendency' of all forms of life. This is a person's internal motivation to develop their potential to the maximum – not just to survive but to make the very best of their existence.

Rogers used the term 'fully-functioning' to describe reaching your best potential. There are five elements of Roger's model:

- openness to experience – listening and understanding

- existential living – living in the 'here-and-now'

- organismic trusting – to trust yourself to do what feels right

- experiential freedom – acknowledging the feeling of freedom, and taking responsibility for choices

- creativity – participating in the actualisation of others and the world as a whole.

Promoting well-being

Both Maslow's hierarchy and Rogers' idea about self-actualisation express the relationship between a person's identity and their self-esteem. If you support a person's health and social needs, such as achieving a feeling of connection and belonging; they can work towards self-esteem, voicing their experience and knowledge and their 'self-actualisation', acceptance, creativity and spiritual fulfilment.

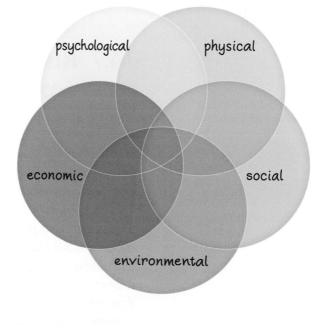

Factors that make up our well-being

Supporting individuals

When working in health and social care roles, everyone has a responsibility to create effective relationships with people using health and social care services. This involves:

- working in partnership with individuals to set realistic and achievable goals

- empowering individuals to develop confidence and feel good about themselves

- creating and maintaining a positive environment to promote the well-being of individuals, for example holding positive attitudes, supporting activities and creating pleasant surroundings

- creating and maintaining positive relationships

- encouraging open communication

- supporting agreed ways of working that contribute to the well-being of individuals and colleagues.

By supporting the person in these ways, you can promote their well-being and the outcomes of the health and social care provided.

14.7 Risk assessment in enabling a person-centred approach

As part of providing person-centred care, you need to develop a positive and enabling approach to communicating risk information. This empowers individuals to make informed decisions in relation to potential and perceived risks and their consequences. You can support individuals in taking an active role in decision making by evaluating and appraising the advantages and disadvantages of their choices. Examples of these choices include lifestyle decisions that affect health, such as smoking, drinking and being overweight. Individuals will need to:

- assess and consider the benefits and drawbacks relating to, for instance, specific investigations or treatment decisions

◗ make use of impartial support in thinking through and calculating the risks involved in surgical procedures, invasive tests and some life-threatening situations

◗ make judgements about decisions relating to their care and support, including long-term care options and end-of-life decisions.

Balancing risk

In Unit 7 you learnt that **risk enablement** is about supporting the person in balancing the risks and benefits of the decisions and choices they are making. Person-centred care means allowing the person to make their choices as independently as possible, supported by relevant and accessible information, and allowing time for the decision-making process. The idea of risk enablement is key to putting the person at the centre of their care. This has to be underpinned by reliable, consistent and trusting relationships and good communication.

Consequences and accountability

Clearly all choices have consequences. Where a person has made a choice with the full information available, and if they have the capacity for decision making, they must be accountable for the consequences. You will experience consequences of the choices you make throughout your life.

Risk taking Enabling and supporting the person to make informed choices and decisions by understanding and taking responsibility for their actions and the consequences.

Risk enablement Getting the balance right between risk taking and being risk averse while paying attention to the issues of safeguarding and the professional's duty of care.

Key Terms

What would you do?

Molly has renal failure (her kidneys do not work). She is a single parent with two young children who she struggles to care for as she spends three afternoons a week at the hospital having dialysis (a machine removes the waste products from her blood as her kidneys are unable to do this). Molly cannot work and receives benefits to support her family but child care and transport costs use up a lot of money. Molly also needs to eat a special diet, which adds to her household costs.

Using the knowledge you have gained so far, make a list of Molly's likely needs for support from the health and social care system.

Lifestyle

Poor lifestyle choices, such as smoking, drinking alcohol and (lack of) exercise, may have an effect on a person's health for several years or decades into the future. People with learning difficulties or mental health issues may need additional support in making sense of information in order to make positive lifestyle choices.

End-of-life care and decisions

End-of-life care helps people with advanced, incurable illnesses to live as well as possible until they die. This is an area where person-centred care planning really matters. The physical and emotional needs of the person and their family are identified and should be met by skilled staff throughout the last phase of the person's life and into bereavement.

End-of-life care planning is particularly important to get right so that the person receives the health and social care support that they need at the time they need it; and doesn't get interventions that they do not want.

find out!

The end-of-life register is a scheme where people who have been identified as nearing the end of their life have their care plan made accessible to a range of local service providers (for example the GP out of hours service, the ambulance service and the community health services). By doing this, information about a person's choices and preferences can be shared easily with others involved in providing care; ensuring that person-centred care can be provided. This idea has been tested in several locations in England. Find out what arrangements are in place in your area for sharing this information at the time it is needed.

Towards the end of their life, a person may choose not to be taken to hospital if their condition gets worse or to have their pain medication increased. These decisions will be worked through with a skilled professional so that the person understands the potential consequences for their well-being and for their family.

Person-centred care for the person with long-term conditions

In Britain, six out of ten adults report having one or more long-term or chronic conditions. Eighty per cent of primary care consultations and two thirds of emergency hospital admissions in the UK are related to long-term conditions. People with long-term conditions also use significant support from social care and voluntary organisations.

The Department of Health's strategy for long-term conditions aims to put people at the centre of decision making about their care, supporting informed choice and giving people control over their lives with particular emphasis on:

- prevention and early intervention
- supported self-care
- personalisation
- personalised care planning
- care close to home.

The strategy requires real partnership working between people with long-term conditions, their carers, the wider community and those who work in health and social care. This requires specific skills and competencies and, in some cases, the design of new roles and innovative solutions.

In order to achieve the best possible experience, people with long-term conditions need:

- support and information to cope with their practical and emotional needs
- support and information to help them manage the long-term and immediate effects of their illness and its treatment
- information in a range of formats to enable them to understand their condition and empower them to take responsibility for its management
- access to regular ongoing support from qualified professionals
- palliative care provided as and when needed and in the setting the person chooses.

find out!

Local support and care for children and young people with a range of emotional, mental health and physical ill-health are normally provided by a mix of social care, health and voluntary organisations. Young people moving between children's and adult services need extra care and attention at this time; find out what arrangements are made for young people transitioning into the service where you work.

People with long-term conditions need special attention to person-centred care planning; they require input from a range of health and social care providers as their needs change.

The most common long-term condition are outlined below.

Cancer

More than one in three people will develop cancer during their lifetime. The number of people living with cancer is increasing because treatments are becoming more successful. In order for treatments to work well, a person-centred approach to joined-up care throughout the patient journey or pathway is essential. This includes timely referral, specialist diagnosis, effective treatments, supported recovery and long-term care for people with cancer.

Heart and circulatory disease

Heart and circulatory disease is the greatest cause of death in Britain and the cost to individuals, health and social care provision and society is significant. By integrating person-centred care throughout the patient journey, the effectiveness of the care and outcomes can be improved. Prevention, early diagnosis, prompt treatment and effective rehabilitation all contribute to maximising the person's quality of life.

Respiratory disease

Respiratory diseases (involving lungs and breathing) often have significant and long-term effects. From asthma in young people to chronic obstructive airways disease (COPD) in older people, the effects can impact the person's well-being and ability to be active. Respiratory diseases respond well to proactive self-management by the individual, supported by high-quality information and skilled professional input. The weather has a big effect on respiratory diseases so innovations such as more accurate weather forecasting and text alerts can help people to manage their own health. This is one example of how a person-centred care plan works in practice.

Diabetes

Nearly three million people are affected by diabetes in the UK. Diabetes has a significant effect on the health and quality of life of an individual because of other long-term complications that can result, especially if the person's diabetes is not well managed. Circulatory disease, neurological and eye conditions can all lead to difficulties with mobility and sight, which in turn may have an impact on the person's ability to work and remain active. Raised blood sugar levels can make infections more serious. Person-centred care underpins a multi-disciplinary approach while care given out of hospital helps the person to manage their health more proactively. Telemedicine for monitoring can be useful.

Musculoskeletal disorders

Musculoskeletal disorders refer to any problems or conditions that may be acute or chronic to do with the muscles or skeletal structure. Chronic pain (often in the back or legs) can accumulate over several years and is attributed to poor manual handling and lifting techniques.

Musculoskeletal disorders can affect people of all ages. They include some progressive long-term conditions and traumatic injuries, and can affect the person's quality of life significantly. Person-centred care offered by health and social care services involves expertise in rehabilitation and use of aids and adaptations to support the person's mobility and independence. The individual may also need practical support and emotional support if they are unable to work or socialise.

Care of people with musculoskeletal disorders

Dementia

One in three people over the age of 65 will develop dementia, and many people have a fear of getting this condition. People with dementia occupy around a quarter of hospital beds; many hospitals struggle to provide the high-quality care that people with dementia need. There are examples of excellent and innovative practice across many care settings.

Whether people are being cared for in their own home, or in care homes, the staff need knowledge and skills to offer person-centred approaches in supporting them to lead as meaningful and fulfilling a life as possible.

People with dementia and their families and friends appreciate good information about health and care services. They also need to be able to give feedback on their experiences.

The document 'Supporting People with Long-term Conditions' was published in January 2005 by the Department of Health; this introduced the NHS and Social Care Model. As you review what you have learnt in this unit, you will realise that the vision set out in this document is for a delivery system similar to that of the American Kaiser Permente model; and that the theme of 'person centredness' runs throughout, with teams of staff working together with people with long-term conditions and their families, supported by specialists.

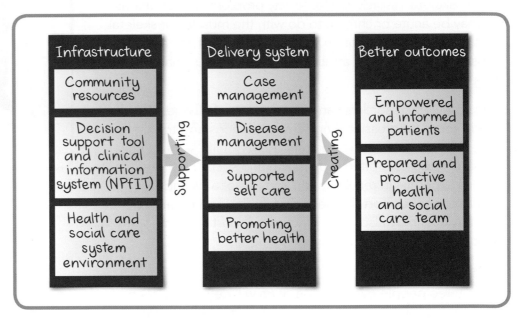

NHS Health and Social Care Model

Some of the principles of the NHS and Social Care Model are:

- making systematic links between health, social care, patients and carers

- identifying everyone with a long-term condition

- categorising people so they can receive care according to their needs

- developing ways to identify people who may become high-intensity individuals

- establishing multi-disciplinary teams in primary care, supported by specialist advice

- developing local ways to support self-care.

Carers for people with dementia often need support. Person-centred care involves assessing and supporting the needs of carers.

More than half a million people in England are the primary care giver for someone with dementia. Those who care for people with dementia are likely to need support. The NICE and SCIE dementia guidelines advise that carers are given access to psychological therapies. Carers have a right to assessment and may choose a personal budget for their support. Where one person is caring for a partner with dementia, the carer may wish to access support for their relationship as a couple.

Advance health care directives, advance directives or 'living wills' are instructions given by an individual regarding decisions about healthcare in the event that they can no longer make those decisions for themselves. This can either be a 'living will where the person leaves instructions for treatment (or withdrawal of treatment) or give power of attorney for someone to make decisions on their behalf.

did you know?

Continuing Healthcare is a package of ongoing care out of hospital that is arranged and funded by the NHS, for people with continuing need for healthcare. The care may be provided at the person's own home or in a care home. People who need continuing healthcare may have a complex health need that requires a lot of care and support, or a condition that needs specialist nursing care. People near to the end of their life are also likely to be eligible.

Continuing Healthcare is subject to a detailed assessment by a skilled health or social care professional, and the need will be reviewed as the person's needs change.

Case study

In Practice

Involving an individual in improvement – a person-centred approach to agreeing goals?

Paul had spent several weeks in an intensive care unit with complex health needs. After this he was exhausted and his recovery, as an inpatient, was slow and discouraging. Paul wanted to go home but struggled to achieve the criteria that was expected for a 'safe discharge'.

A few months later Paul agreed to take part in a large, multi-disciplinary service improvement (redesign) event. The hospital had realised that too many patients were staying in hospital for too long and wanted to find ways to change this. The event attracted a range of professionals from many areas. Everyone was clear about their goals for Paul's safe transfer out of intensive care and going home. Paul had to eat 2000 calories a day; walk up 15 steps; have blood results within specified limits; have someone available to collect him; have all his medications ready; and leave before midday so that the next person could use the bed.

What became clear as Paul told his story was that he had never expressed his goal to anyone. Paul wanted to go home and was willing to make sacrifices to do this.

He wanted to go to the golf club and see his friends and start to get back to normal.

Paul told us that he eventually left hospital. That evening he slowly climbed the stairs to his bedroom; when he reached the top he was so exhausted he fell asleep on the floor. The next morning he went to the golf club knowing that he was on the way to getting back to normal.

Everyone in the room realised that understanding and sharing Paul's goal – to get home and back to the golf club – would have helped them work in a more joined-up way, and would most likely have achieved the goal more quickly. Everyone agreed to make the required improvements to goal planning.

Paul focused on achieving his goal

Websites for further research

www.dhsspsni.gov.uk (Department of Health, Social services and Public Safety)

www.local.gov.uk (Local Government Improvement and Development in the Local Government Association website)

www.bbc.co.uk (search for 'social care': social care – how the system works)

Quick Quiz

1 Which of the following is a reasonable description of person-centred care?
   a. Putting the person and their family at the centre of the care planning
   b. Making sure that the person can balance correctly when they walk
   c. Making sure that their benefits are being paid
   d. Prioritising their appointment at the outpatient clinic

2 In Life Story work, which of the following would not be a useful medium for recording the person's memories?
   a. A computer file
   b. A scrap book
   c. A memory box buried in the garden
   d. A box of selected photographs

3 Which of the following activities would not contribute to person-centred decision making?
   a. The information and advice they need about options
   b. Taking the person for a walk in the park
   c. Respecting their right to nominate a third party to make decisions
   d. Giving the person time to make decisions

4 Which of the following methods may help an individual to give consent if they lack capacity?
   a. Asking their relatives
   b. Using physical or communication aids
   c. Speaking up as their advocate
   d. Asking them to make a decision straight away

5 In which of the following situations would you not expect to be supported by a senior colleague?
   a. Bereavement
   b. Threatening, frightening or violent behaviour
   c. Supporting privacy
   d. Incidents that are likely to have personal consequences such as those involving confidential information

6 Which of the following behaviours is not associated with depression?
   a. Being withdrawn
   b. Eating a poor diet
   c. Poor personal hygiene
   d. Confusion and disorientation

7 Which of the following services would not necessarily be included in a palliative care package?
   a. Pain control
   b. Attention to any advance directives or living will that the person may have chosen to make
   c. Counselling
   d. Accommodation in a hospice

8 Which of the following is not a theory of motivation?
   a. Instinct
   b. Hunger
   c. Arousal
   d. Humanistic

9 Which of the following is not a potential complication of diabetes?
   a. Alcohol abuse
   b. Blood circulation problems in the lower leg and foot
   c. Problems with eyesight
   d. Infections

10 Which of the following is not provided by Continuing Healthcare?
   a. Free healthcare in the person's own home
   b. Free healthcare in a residential home
   c. Specialist nursing care in a residential home
   d. Acupuncture

Understand
health and safety in
adult social care settings

This unit provides the knowledge and understanding of a comprehensive range of health and safety issues and responsibilities that you must be aware of. It also explains agreed ways of working compliant with legislation.

On completion of this unit you should:

- know the different responsibilities relating to health and social care settings
- know the importance of risk assessments and their relation to health and safety
- know the procedures for responding to accidents and sudden illness
- know how to reduce the spread of infection
- know how to move and handle equipment and other objects safely
- know the principles of assisting and moving an individual
- know how to handle hazardous substances
- know how to promote environmental safety procedures in the social care setting
- know how to manage stress
- know the procedures regarding the handling of medication
- know how to handle and store food safely

15.1 Your responsibilities relating to health and safety care settings

Legislation relating to health and safety in a social care setting

There are some key items of health and safety legislation that must be considered in relation to social care settings.

The Health and Safety at Work Act (1974)

This Act provided a basis for all aspects of health and safety within a workplace to ensure that employers, employees, visitors and the environment in which they work is at all times safe and provides a basis for optimum health and safety requirements. Employers must provide written policies if they employ five or more people. Employees have a duty to cooperate with agreed ways of working and to keep themselves and others safe.

List four health and safety requirements from the Health and Safety at Work Act (1974) that are needed for health and safety within a workplace.

The Management of Health and Safety at Work Regulations (1999)

These regulations introduced the concept of risk assessing before carrying out any activities that may present risks to health or safety. Activities can involve the environment, the individuals who are being cared for, visitors and the staff carrying out workplace duties.

The Manual Handling Operations Regulations (1992)

It is a legal requirement for employers and employees to follow certain steps of risk assessing to reduce the risk of injury to

There is a balance between independence, well-being and risk avoidance

themselves and the individuals they care for. If possible, you should avoid any hazardous manoeuvre that may cause injury. When this is not possible, the risks have to be assessed using the TILE acronym:

T = TASK. What is involved in the task, for example is there any lifting, stooping, twisting, pulling or pushing?

I = THE INDIVIDUAL. Think about the weight of the person, their height, age and general health as well as any physical limitations such as a plaster cast or a prosthesis.

L = THE LOAD. Will the person or load be bulky and difficult to lift and manoeuvre?

E = THE ENVIRONMENT. What space is available to make the move and are there any fixed objects or slippery surfaces? Where is the destination and is it easy to approach?

The risk assessments are focused on **ergonomics**. This simply means a way of fitting the task to the person.

As with any other task, obtain consent to move someone in a certain way or to use equipment.

> **Ergonomics** Fitting a task to the individual, their capabilities, strength, stability and mental capacity. It can involve the use of aids.
>
> **Key Term**

Health and Safety (First Aid) Regulations (1981)

This Act enforces workplaces to ensure that some of their staff are qualified to administer first aid and that qualifications are renewed every three years. The Health and Safety Commission and Executive (HSC/E) currently hold regulatory responsibility for monitoring this.

Reporting of Injuries, Diseases and Dangerous Occurrences (RIDDOR)

It is a legal requirement to report any serious injuries, diseases (such as meningitis), deaths and long-term illnesses to the HSC/E or to Environmental Health. There has recently been a change in the requirements, which requires employers to report when employees are absent from work for seven days due to an injury.

Control of Substances Hazardous to Health (COSHH)

This Act enforces safety rules for storing any hazardous substances such as cleaning fluids, dangerous chemicals and medicines. It also includes the safe use of these substances and the management of spillages and disposal. This also includes storing, administering and disposing of medicines.

Care workers should never use any hazardous substance without knowing what it is, its use and the safe disposal method.

find out !

Find out about the standards that relate to health and safety by visiting www.cqc.org.uk and www.dh.gov.uk

Health and safety policies and procedures that protect those in health and social care settings

Policies and procedures are based on current legislation and ensure that managers, employers and employees work to agreed standards. These are in place to protect the staff as well as residents or patients and visitors.

When you begin work in a health and social care setting, you follow an induction process that addresses all aspects of health and safety. These include:

- infection control
- first aid
- food hygiene
- health and safety (risk assessing)
- fire procedures
- manual handling techniques
- emergency situations
- medication handling.

think about

Think about the induction procedures in a school or a college. How good are they at promoting the health and safety of all students and staff? What rules exist and could they be better or more helpful towards certain groups of people?

Match the legislation with the task in the right-hand column of the table below.

1 COSHH	A Checking the identity of individuals before giving them any tablets
2 RIDDOR	B Renewing your first aid qualification
3 Health and Safety (First Aid) Reguations (1981)	C Hand washing and wearing disposable gloves to change a soiled sheet and washing hands after placing sheet in red aliginate bag and disposing of gloves into clinical waste container.
4 Management of Health and Safety (1999)	D Obtaining consent from an individual to use the hoist and checking it is in good working order.
5 Manual Handling Operations	E Conducting a risk assessment before taking a frail client to the shower.
6 Infection Control Guidelines (Department of Health)	F Checking the 'use by' dates on deliveries of fresh cooked chicken.
7 The Food Hygiene (England) Reguations (2006)	G Reporting an accident in the setting
8 The Handling of Medicines in Social Care Settings Guidance (2007)	H Checking the manufacturer's instructions to use new disinfectant
9 Regulations Reform (Fire Safety) Order (2005)	I De-cluttering the tops of cupboards from combustable material.

Every day and during every shift, you will need to look out for any potential hazard and be prepared to take action. Sometimes this will involve calling for help or seeking advice from your manager but you should never leave a situation that is unsafe if you are not sure what you should do. Always remember that you are accountable for your actions.

Differences in the main health and safety responsibilities of different roles

There are differences in the main health and safety responsibilities of different roles, as outlined below.

The social care worker

When you sign your contract, you agree to ways of working that will meet health and safety standards. That means that you must familiarise yourself with policies and procedures, update yourself on the necessary knowledge and understanding required and carry out your tasks competently. **Never attempt to perform a task that you have not been trained to do.**

The employer or manager

It is your employer's or manager's duty to make sure that you are introduced to the policies and procedures of the setting, receive the necessary and mandatory training in all topic areas, ideally within six weeks and your manager should also be accessible for your queries and to guide you.

You will not be able to do some tasks until you have been practically assessed on them, such as the handling of medication and food handling. Your manager will confirm when you are competent and may suggest further and specialised training.

In your organisation what is defined as 'specialised training'?

Others in the social care setting

Other people may be health professionals, visitors and those receiving care within the setting. Everyone has to be aware of certain policies and procedures that protect the environment and the people within it. One example is 'No smoking'.

When responsibility for health and safety lies with the individual

Visitors to nursing homes, residential care and hospitals are advised to wash their hands on entry and to use an alcohol gel. Posters promote hand washing, not sitting on beds or using residents' toilets in order to prevent infections.

List three other rules in addition to 'NO SMOKING' policies for visiting health professionals and others that comply with health and safety.

Hygiene is important for both employees and visitors to a nursing home, residential care home or hospital

Another potential hazard is storing cooked food for residents at the wrong temperature and in unhygienic situations.

What posters, signage, rules and guidance exist in residential care homes, nursing care and the community to encourage responsibility for health and safety?

'You have that nice bit of fish later when you feel better'

Take a walk around your school or college and evaluate the measures taken to promote and protect health and safety. Look at the signs and access points and try to critically analyse health and safety aspects of the environment in which you study.

Specific tasks that should only be carried out with special training

Carers who are not trained to carry out specialised tasks run the danger of harming individuals in their care. As all carers are accountable for their actions, the consequences could be dismissal and a sanction on the home: meaning, it could close down.

What would you do?

Imagine that you are asked to take a frail woman to the toilet but you have not completed any training on manual handling or risk assessing. What would you do?

Imagine that you are asked to give someone a nebuliser but you have never heard of it. What would you do?

The dangers of performing tasks for which you have received no training could be very serious for the individuals in your care.

Health and safety – a UK local authority

The health and safety of both our individuals and our staff is one of our key concerns. We offer training to staff to help them to undertake new tasks successfully, and it is important to remember not to take on any tasks that you have not been trained for. The consequences of handling hazardous substances or medication without training can be serious, not only for you but for others around you.

Where to get support and information about health and safety

Never be afraid of asking for guidance and support. Your manager and senior workers are there to help you. You can also speak to visiting health professionals and ask to work shadow people. You can access websites, policies, procedures and guidance to help you with the required knowledge.

It is useful to make notes in a reflective learning diary and make sure that you follow up on queries. Unanswered queries tend to return later so the earlier you seek advice the better.

A benefit of this practice is that it also serves as useful evidence for your assessor or your own development (see Unit 11).

15.2 Know the importance of risk assessments

Why is it important to assess health and safety risks?

If you do not assess the risks in your workplaces with regard to health and safety and the activities that you perform, you are in breach of the law. It is very likely that you could cause harm to those whose care is your principal duty.

Assess the risk

Steps to carrying out a risk assessment

There are five standard steps to carrying out a risk assessment:

1. Identify the hazard.

2. Decide who may be at risk of harm and how.

3. Evaluate the risks; decide on how to reduce them

4. Record the findings.

5. Review the risk assessments, change if necessary.

How to address potential health and safety risks

There are many potential health and safety risks within a setting. You could consider the environment, the routines within a day and the individuals in your care.

The key issue is to identify the potential risks, remove the hazards and so avoid any injuries or harm.

How risk assessments can help address dilemmas between an individual's rights and health and safety concerns

Risk assessments are intended to prevent anything that may cause harm. When you carry out a risk assessment, individuals can see that this is for the benefit of their own health and safety. There will be times when you will encounter individuals who want to manage their lifestyles in a way that does not meet general health and safety guidelines. If someone wants to smoke or take recreational drugs, overeat when they are obese, or never take any exercise, you do not have a right to make them change. You do, however, have a duty of care to highlight potential hazards to individuals and if they decide to take risks with their health then you have at least given them the information to make the right choice. This information and the decision of the individual must be recorded. You must also record how the decision and any plans will be implemented and monitored.

find out!

Describe three environmental risks, three risks to do with a routine, such as mealtimes, three risks of a medicine round and three risks with the personal care and mobility of residents. Then devise four ways to reduce the risks for each category.

What would you do?

A resident wants to be independent and take his medication with his meals in his own room. In the past, he has left his tablets in the sitting room and started to smoke in his room. You know he has rights to be independent and choose his actions – so what do you do?

Promoting health and safety within the social care setting

You must be aware and understand how to continually promote health and safety within your setting. There are a few ways that this can be done.

- In your day-to-day duties, observe individuals and encourage them to adhere to policies such as no smoking, closing doors behind them, letting staff know if they are going for a walk and informing staff whether they are experiencing any difficulties with walking, toileting, taking medication, eating or drinking.

- Get into the habit of observing the environment and making sure that areas are safe to be in.

- Observe frequent visitors (so that you can spot a strange visitor) and encourage all visitors to adhere to security arrangements such as signing a register, washing hands and not sitting on beds.

- Check that posters encouraging security, fire protection and evacuation (including labelled fire exits) are clear.

- Check that posters promote hand hygiene and describe with pictures the recommended procedure for hand washing.

- Check that individuals have clean clothes to wear and that personal hygiene is maintained.

think about...

Consider three aspects that tell you a sluice area is maintained hygienically.

Describe four things to check to ensure the safety of a sitting room.

15.3 Responding to accidents and sudden illness

Accidents and sudden illness that may occur in a social care setting

Sudden illness usually requires a a carer to follow organisational procedures very quickly. Someone's life may be at risk.

Although it is not your responsibility to diagnose a condition, it is your responsibility to respond to sudden illness and so you must be able to recognise the common signs and symptoms, which can include the following:

- shortness of breath with possible accompanying blueness (cyanosis) around the lips, fingertips and earlobes.

- complaints of chest pain

- signs of shock such as pale and clammy skin, complaints of nausea and/or dizziness

- disorientation, lethargy or drowsiness

- a drooping mouth and a fall away of the arm on one side (sudden paralysis) – this suggests a stroke and needs immediate attention.

These are all signs of a serious condition and need the attention of medical personnel.

Consider two other types of accidents that can occur within a health and social care setting.

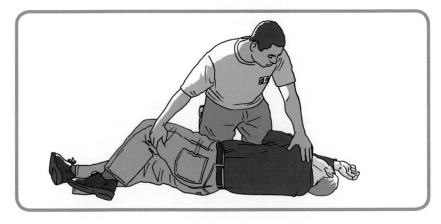

If a person is having breathing difficulties, place in the recovery position and stay with them until help arrives. See page 144 for more information

Procedures to be followed if an accident or sudden illness occurs

You should be familiar with the procedures to follow in the event of a serious accident or sudden illness. You should also attend a first aid course. The basic procedure to follow (if someone has collapsed) is based on an acronym:

D R S A B C

1   Check for any DANGERS and remove them.

2   Check the RESPONSE of that person (by shouting and shaking their shoulders lightly).

3   SHOUT for help.

4   Check the AIRWAY (by tilting the chin back).

5   Check for BREATHING (no more than ten seconds).

6   Check for CIRCULATION (look at colour and movements). C can also mean **CPR** (if there is no breathing call 999, or get someone to do this for you and commence CPR).

7   Currently CPR consists of opening the airway, lifting the chin, checking for breathing and, if this is not present, you must do 30 chest compressions followed by 2 breaths. Please note that this is the adult procedure only; babies and children require breaths initially before chest compressions.

8   If there is breathing and you see a pink colour (indicating a circulation), then you must put the person on their side (recovery position) if you have been trained and stay with the person until help arrives. This is the recovery position.

Although CPR may help to restart a heart that has stopped beating, the main concern is the delivery of oxygen to the brain. The cells of a brain starved of oxygen will die and not regenerate. This is why it is important to act speedily in response to cardiac arrest.

Bleeding is also classed as an emergency situation but your main priority is whether the person is breathing or conscious. If there is a haemorrhage you must apply pressure to the wound, elevate the wound above the level of the heart and press firmly.

Ninety-five per cent of major slips and trips in social care settings result in broken bones. Most slips occur on wet or contaminated floors. (www.hse.gov.uk/healthservices) The research suggests that these accidents are due to poor housekeeping, wet floors and not always cleaning up spillages straightaway.

CPR CPR means Cardio-Pulmonary Resuscitation (Cardio refers to the heart, pulmonary refers to the lungs and resuscitation is to recover the breathing and circulatory cycle).

Cardiac arrest This means the heart has stopped beating.

Key Terms

Case study

In Practice

Miriam, a new care worker, has just completed a first aid course. As she assists Mrs Dyson back to her room after tea, she notices that she appears dazed, looks pale and feels clammy to touch.

Miriam shouts for help and, getting a cushion, places Mrs Dyson gently on the floor, raising her legs. She then covers her with a blanket and asks her colleague to get the manager and call a doctor.

When Mrs Dyson does not respond to her questions, she places her in the recovery position and stays with her, monitoring her breathing and colour.

She tells the paramedics exactly what happened and then makes a written report of the incident.

What would you do?

You are called by a cleaner to check a resident who has been complaining of indigestion and she says he now 'looks bluey grey and is not responding'.

find out!

In this case study, why did Miriam place Mrs Dyson on the floor and raise her legs?
What is a recovery position and when is it used?

The importance of emergency first aid tasks being carried out by qualified first aiders

If you attempted an emergency first aid procedure that you were not trained for, you could harm the person. For example, moving someone who has a broken limb may cause further damage and applying a bandage too tightly may cause a lack of important blood flow to the area. If you do not understand the recovery position or CPR, you may not do anything at all but vital time will have been wasted if you are the first on the scene. In order to feel competent, you must attend a first aid course. Your manager should arrange for this as part of your induction.

15.4 **Know how to reduce the spread of infection**

Key Terms

Pathogenic bacteria These are harmful bacteria that can make us ill.

Vulnerable groups These include older people, babies and children, pregnant women and people with low resistance to infections, sometimes referred to as 'immuno-compromised'.

did you know?

Infections are transmitted via cycles or chains of infection.

Infections happen because **pathogenic bacteria** (or viruses) spread and may affect **vulnerable groups** more than others.

Pathogenic bacteria and viruses are types of micro-organisms and can be transmitted via:

- droplets or airborne infections (breathed in)
- direct contact with another person
- indirect contact (from contaminated objects)
- ingestion (being eaten)
- the bloodstream (contaminated needles or bites and stings or due to septicaemia)
- an ascending infection (up the reproductive and urinary tract).

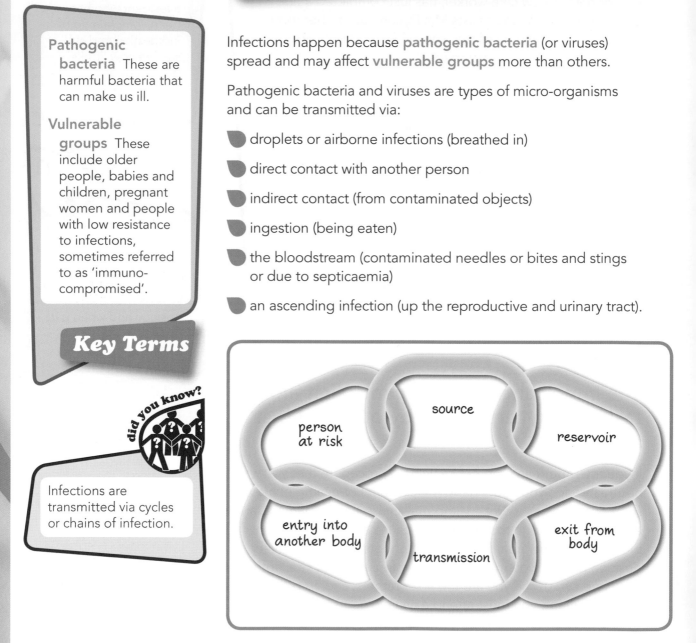

Only one link of the chain of infection needs to be broken to prevent infection

Hand washing

Hand washing is probably the simplest and most important task you can do to help the prevention of infection. Follow the Department of Health's five-step recommended procedure:

1   Wet your hands under running water.

2   Apply liquid soap thoroughly.

3   Lather and scrub, ensuring to wash between the fingers, the tips of the fingers and the thumb, the front and back of hands.

4   Rinse thoroughly.

5   Dry using a paper towel or an air dryer. Dispose of paper towel using a pedal-operated bin.

Your personal hygiene

You must get into the habit of washing your hands thoroughly each time you start a new task, complete a task or handle a soiled item. This is in addition to wearing disposable gloves. You can use gel if you are not near a wash basin but this is no substitute for good hand washing.

think about

> Consider three other occasions when you must wash your hands.

did you know?

> Alcohol gel is not effective against the troublesome bacterium, Clostridium Difficile, or the viral causes of gastro enteritis.

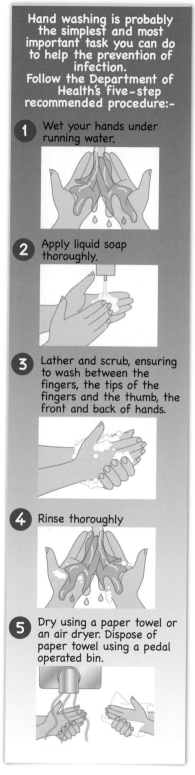

Hand washing is probably the simplest and most important task you can do to help the prevention of infection. Follow the Department of Health's five-step recommended procedure:-

1   Wet your hands under running water.

2   Apply liquid soap thoroughly.

3   Lather and scrub, ensuring to wash between the fingers, the tips of the fingers and the thumb, the front and back of hands.

4   Rinse thoroughly

5   Dry using a paper towel or an air dryer. Dispose of paper towel using a pedal operated bin.

The five-step handwashing procedure

General cleanliness is also important so you need to check your oral hygiene, ensure that your body is free from odours and sweat, that your nails are kept short and clean and hair is tied back if it's long. Cover sores or lesions on your hands with waterproof dressings. Cover coughs and sneezes with your hand and use disposable tissues. If you have a cold, cough or high temperature, you should not go to work where you will be in contact with vulnerable people. Similarly, you should stay away from work if you have a stomach bug (diarrhoea and/or vomiting).

Encouraging the individual's personal hygiene

Residents and patients in care homes or nursing homes need to be reminded to wash their hands before meals, when receiving medication and after using the toilet. You can prompt them by offering their washcloth, wet wipes and a paper towel if their mobility is poor.

Make sure that the individuals you care for have soap and shampoo, toothpaste, clean towels, hair brushes and combs and clean clothes.

You should check that wet items are left to dry and not put away wet or damp, which makes them smell and encourages bacteria.

Your role in supporting others to follow practices that reduce the spread of infection

It is everyone's responsibility to help reduce the possible spread of infection. In hospitals, there are signs encouraging visitors to wash their hands before entering a ward and to use alcohol gel. They are also discouraged from sitting on the beds. Posters and information about infection control should be prominent in all health and social care settings. You should observe general practices to ensure that the risks of infection are kept to a minimum.

As a team member, ensure that you attend training at least every year and discuss any measures with colleagues to keep your organisation clean and free from germs.

Your working areas should show posters of effective hand washing as a reminder to all, including visiting health professionals.

It is important to use non-touch techniques and wear disposable gloves, preferably non-latex. Remember to wear gloves and aprons when disposing of soiled items, clinical waste and household waste.

find out!

How does the setting in which you work promote the control and prevention of infection?

15.5 Moving and handling equipment and other objects safely

The main points of legislation that relate to moving and handling

Remember that the Health and Safety at Work Act (1974) sets out responsibilities for the employer and the employee to keep themselves safe by following agreed procedures. The Manual Handling Operations Regulations (1992) set out a series of steps that organisations should follow:

1   Avoid all tasks that may involve the risk of injury.

2   If the lifting or manoeuvre must be carried out, assess the risk of injury using TILE (see page 134):

A related piece of legislation is the Management of Health and Safety at Work Regulations (1999). This sets out legal requirements that all potentially unsafe activities are pre-assessed using risk assessments. The five steps for risk assessing are outlined above on page 141.

> **❝** In health and social care services, moving and handling injuries account for 40 per cent of work-related sickness absence. Around 5,000 moving and handling injuries are reported each year in health services and around 2,000 in social care. **❞**

www.hse.gov.uk

Principles for safe moving and handling

You must adhere to workplace guidelines for risk assessing and following the principles for safe moving and handling. The key things to remember are:

▶ Avoid lifting manually unless you have no alternative.

▶ Check the care plan for the lifting and handling advice.

▶ Conduct a risk assessment using the TILE approach.

▶ Obtain the assistance of your colleagues and engage the individual in supporting you by helping themselves to move if at all possible.

▶ Ensure that the manoeuvre does not put anyone at risk of injury or harm.

What would you do?

Harriet is 91 and has slipped to the floor, knocking over a jug of juice, which has pooled around her as well as making her very wet.

1 Identify the risks.

2 Who may be harmed and how?

3 How do you assess the risks to reduce the possibility of further harm to Harriet or yourself? What would you do if this happened to you?

4 What will you record?

5 How will this situation need to be monitored and reviewed?

Situations that may require additional support

Some situations will require you to consider the use of mechanical aids such as a hoist and slings. These can be mobile or fixed (for example in a bathroom).

A monkey pole or rope ladder that is anchored to the bottom of the bed can provide support for the individual to sit further up or straight up in bed. Individuals will need to be able to use their upper limbs.

Handling belts are placed around an individual's waist. These have handles and assist with transfers from bed to chair and chair to bed but are only useful when individuals have some ability to help themselves. They are not a lifting aid, however.

Slipper slide sheets can assist with turning in bed. You must make sure that you use two or three and hold them during the operation with a strong grip.

Similarly, for transfers there are banana boards, which individuals slide onto and glide across to another surface (ideally of the same height).

Additional supportive equipment may include the type of bed that is best suited to a large or immobile individual. Bariatrics is a specialist approach for obese people whereby specialist lifting equipment will be required and specialised training needed.

Think about the most suitable support methods for the individuals you care for and ask them what helps them the most.

What aids and equipment are used in your setting? Research others using the internet. Do you know how to use them?

Moving and handling tasks must only be carried out after specialist training

In all cases of lifting and handling you will need the correct training, especially when operating a hoist or using any other type of specialised techniques or equipment. Following training, you must be assessed as competent.

Poor manual handling techniques can lead to musculoskeletal disorders, which can be severely disabling in later life (see page 127). Particularly hazardous actions are:

- lifting from the floor
- sudden twisting
- sudden jerking
- bending over from the waist
- straining over some distance away from the body
- lifting down heavy objects from above.

Specialised training will show you how to lift correctly, using the correct posture, to look after your body.

People who have lifted objects for years may suddenly suffer a prolapsed disc or sciatica, or sprains and strains. To try to prevent such injuries and disabilities, the Manual Handling Regulations introduced steps that all employers had to put in place for people who have to lift and manoeuvre objects (or people).

Remember that it is a legal requirement for your employer or manager to conduct risk assessments and to engage competent and trained staff.

You are accountable for your actions – so if you cause an injury or harm to someone, you may receive disciplinary action.

If you injure yourself and the proper control measures have not been taken, you cannot expect any compensation.

15.6 The principles of assisting and moving an individual

Why is it important to have specialist training before assisting and moving an individual?

Individuals in your care are very different from objects that do not move, change their shape or wave their arms about! Ergonomics is an approach that, following assessment, fits the task to the individual. Always be aware that people who are moved and handled by others feel a loss of control and need to be able to trust their carers.

In addition to instability, the general condition of the individual needs to be considered. This might include a specific illness, delicate skin, tiredness, injuries, inflexibility or inability to weight bear, pain, obesity or extreme anxiety.

Case study

In Practice

Carer Adam needs to sit Mr Treharne up in bed so that he can have his inhaler. Mr Treharne is 23 stone and short of breath.

Adam checks the care plan and asks a colleague to help him. He obtains consent for the move from Mr Treharne and Adam explains how he will be moved. He also asks Mr Treharne to use his own arms to help and to flex his knees in the bed. He is able to do this. The carers get close to him, one each side to support him but not to manually lift. If this technique no longer worked, it would need to be reviewed and the use of other aids considered.

The 'load' (person) is your biggest priority when risk assessing the transfer or mobility of an individual. The most appropriate way to move them should be documented in the handling care plan. You also need to seek consent to move an individual and respect their decision if they do not want to be moved at the time that suits you. Also consider any pain that a person might experience and ensure that this is controlled before you make it worse with your movements.

Do not move someone who is short of breath unless it is essential. Similarly, ensure that toilet needs are not urgent before you make a transfer such as from bed to chair.

Note that care plans can change because an individual's circumstances may change. If skin conditions worsen, or a person's level of health deterioriates, then their level of ability to participate and engage in moving procedures becomes more difficult. Reviews are therefore ae essential to maintain a level of support that the individual needs.

find out !

Research what medical conditions make moving difficult. Consider the individuals in your setting who have conditions that may be made worse by moving and being handled.

think about

Think about the factors you need to consider for some of the individuals in your workplace. Consider the actions that need to be taken to reduce the possibility of harm or injury.

What might happen if you move an individual without specialist training?

Without specialist training, carers may not fully assess a situation and could cause a lot of harm to individuals or themselves. The risks are threefold:

- You might not use the right posture and lifting technique and could damage your back.

- You might injure the individual.

- You will place the setting in which you work in a vulnerable position if there is a claim for liability.

You would be in breach of the Care Standards Act (2000), the Essential Standards for Quality and Safety (2010) and the Management of Health and Safety (1999) because you will not have risk assessed the situation or followed the care plan.

Consequences of not following an individual's care plan

You are not following your duty of care if you do not involve the people you are moving and handling.

Hopefully you can empathise with individuals who have restricted mobility and can appreciate the loss of control and dignity many will experience, especially if they are not consulted.

People have different preferences for being handled and you must listen to these, evaluate the success of a manoeuvre and prepare to review and change it if necessary.

If you do not follow simple rules, you may cause harm to the individual and this will also have an effect on your relationships with them.

think about

Imagine this: how would you feel if you had no choice about being moved by someone else, if they did not respect your wishes and hurt you by insensitive handling?

15.7 Handling hazardous substances

Types of hazardous substances that may be found in the social care setting

The Control of Substances Hazardous to Health (COSHH) Regulations (2002) set out requirements for employers to prevent or control exposure to any substance that may cause harm.

This includes cleaning fluids and disinfectants, corrosives (containing acid), flammable substances (solvents), pesticides, clinical waste (containing some biological agents), used needles (contaminated with blood), soiled dressings (contaminated with blood and body fluid), any bodily fluids (blood, faeces, vomit, sputum). It also includes medicines, oral medications, liquid medications and preparations for injection into the body.

Hazard symbol	Hazard classification
T+ or T	**Very Toxic (T+) / Toxic (T)** Chemicals that, in very low quantities, cause death or acute or chronic damage to health when inhaled, swallowed or absorbed through the skin.
Xn	**Harmful** Chemicals that may cause death or acute or chronic damage to health.
C	**Corrosive** Chemicals that on contact with living tissues may destroy them.
Xi	**Irritant** Non-corrosive chemicals that through immediate, prolonged or repeated contact with the skin or mucous membranes, may cause inflammation.

Hazard symbol	Hazard classification
E	**Explosive** Chemicals that may react producing heat without atmospheric oxygen, quickly producing gases and that can detonate and explode.
O	**Oxidising** Chemicals that give rise to heat producing reactions when in contact with other substances, particularly flammable substances.
F+ or F	**Flammable** **Extremely (F+)**: Liquids that have an extremely low flash point (below 0°C) and low boiling point (equal to or below 35°C). Or gaseous substances that are flammable in contact with air at ambient temperature and pressure. **Highly (F)**: Chemicals that may become hot and catch fire in contact with air at ambient temperature without any application of energy. A solid that readily catches fire with minimal contact with a source of ignition and that continues to burn after the source is removed. Liquids with a very low flashpoint (equal to or less than 21°C) and not classified as extremely flammable.

Common hazard classifications

find out!

What types of hazardous substances can you identify in your setting and how are these stored?

Storing hazardous substances

It is very important to follow the manufacturer's guidelines for safe storage. Some items should not be stored near others and you must note any incompatibility. Some must be kept at a particular temperature. You must check the labels of all **bio-hazards** for safety advice and note the expiry date.

Your setting will also have guidelines for storing substances and you must closely follow these. You should never ever pour hazardous liquids into other unlabelled bottles or sprays.

Bio-hazards Anything that is biologically hazardous to people or the environment.

Key Term

What would you do?

You have started work in a new small residential unit for people with learning difficulties. They have access to the kitchen but you discover that the cleaner stores the bleach and cleaning materials in the same cupboard as cups, saucers and tea plates. What would you do?

Using hazardous substances

If you are cleaning, it is important to read the instructions on the label. Dilution strengths differ with different products and you must always dilute according to instructions.

You may be required to use PPE, to wear disposable gloves and aprons. Never inhale fumes or get the substance near your eyes. Always wash your hands afterwards – even if you were wearing gloves.

It is also good practice to seal off an area if cleaning. Floors should not be walked on until they are completely dry and 'non-slippy'.

The safe handling of medicines involves many aspects relating to the administering of various medications requiring different routes. You should ask your manager whether you can do a 'Safe Handling of Medicines' course and ensure that you fully understand how to store and administer medications before attempting to do so. You must be assessed as competent by your manager.

The correct cleaning procedures for bathrooms and toilets by searching on the internet, for example on YouTube.

Disposing of hazardous substances

You have some key responsibilities to consider when disposing of hazardous substances:

- Ensure that you have knowledge and awareness of the potential harm that can be caused by careless disposal.

- Use safe hygienic practices that involve the use of PPE (gloves and aprons) and wash hands after the gloves and aprons have been disposed of.

- Complete records that may be required (as in the case of controlled drugs and other drugs that have expired).

- Clinical waste, such as that from a nursing home as opposed to a personal and residential care home, must be registered with a licensed waste disposal company that can treat potentially hazardous biological waste. This kind of waste is placed in yellow clinical bags.

- Put used needles into a sharps box, which should never be more than two-thirds full when sealed.

- Needlestick injury may result in a blood-borne infection such as Hepatitis B.

- Never pour liquids down the sink but return them to the pharmacy with other medications that are no longer required.

Describe two possible hazards to people and the environment if waste disposal was careless.

Describe how you would (in your own setting) dispose of the following items:

1 Soiled linen

2 Sharps

3 Sputum containers

4 Blood on an oxygen mask

5 Some tablets that are brought in with a resident that are two years out of date.

Ensure sharps containers are no more than two-thirds full

Never pour liquid medicines down a sink or drain

15.8 Promoting environmental safety procedures in the social care setting

Fire prevention

The Regulatory Reform (Fire Safety) Order (2005) sets out principles for risk assessments and prevention of fires. It is a legal requirement for all workplaces to clearly display the actions required in the event of a fire and to have in place the most appropriate fire extinguishers and other items, such as fire hoses, smoke alarms and blankets. All workplaces should keep fire doors closed and free from clutter. Storage of combustible items should be kept to a minimum and walkways should also be clear.

Staff should attend fire lectures once a year and be aware of the extinguishers on site and how to use them. All staff should be aware of the evacuation procedure and where the assembly point is.

Other fire prevention actions are that electrical items are tested once a year and residents and visitors are not allowed to smoke on the premises.

Managing a fire

A basic procedure is as follows:

- Raise the alarm.
- Dial 999.
- Prepare for evacuation to the assembly point.
- If possible, use the correct extinguisher on a small fire.
- Ensure that those who are mobile are evacuated quickly and there are sufficient staff to support those who are not able to move unaided.
- Check with any registers the number and names of people assembled.
- Do not return to the building until a fire officer gives permission.

Gas leak prevention

The manager should ensure that gas appliances are checked at least once a year. Emergency numbers in the event of a smell of gas should be displayed.

In the event of a gas leak

You must familiarise yourself with the procedure in the event of a gas leak. It is important to evacuate just as for a fire, helping those with mobility problems and guiding others who are mobile. You will need to make sure that there are no naked flames or inflammable liquids in the vicinity.

Floods

If you are able to evacuate safely then you must do so, following the guidelines of the setting. If you are able to stop water from entering a room then do so. The main potential hazard is electrical items – if equipment is in use it must be turned off if water is liable to impact the current.

Intrusion and security breach prevention

Security of a home is essential and there are ways to ensure this is maintained:

- All staff and visiting personnel should wear identification badges.

- Security codes should be on external doors and perhaps staff should carry a fob for internal doors.

- Safety locks should be on all windows.

- Security personnel should be employed, especially at night.

- Alarm systems must be well maintained.

- All staff must be vigilant when observing any stranger or any display of odd behaviour on the premises and must be prepared to report it.

In the event of an intrusion

If people are seen on the premises who look suspicious, you must report this. Sometimes there are unwelcome visitors to a nursing or residential care home. It is better to stop them coming in rather than allowing unwanted visitors free access. It is important to ask all visitors to sign a book and indicate who they have come to see.

In addition to this, it is good practice to obtain permission from the resident for someone to visit them. You should also respect their right to refuse to see a visitor.

Never confront a stranger but call for help. If any violence or disruption occurs, you must ring the police.

Encouraging others to adhere to environmental safety procedures

When general visitors, healthcare professionals and tradespeople enter the building, they will use the intercom but once inside must be aware of the 'house rules' such as signing in, being escorted and signing out.

Visitors such as trainers who are on site for any length of time must be made aware of the fire evacuation procedures and that smoking is not permissible in any public buildings.

How do you allow freedom while ensuring the security of a building?

One of your residents who has Alzheimer's disease tends to wander off into the garden at all times of day and night. How will you involve colleagues in maintaining her right to go into the garden while mainitaining the security of the home?

Emergency plans to deal with unforeseen incidents

An emergency can cause panic and anxiety, especially among residents who are vulnerable, frail and perhaps insecure. It is very important to have plans in place that involve key people with the expertise to deal with emergencies such as fires, gas leaks, floods and security breaches and who need to be on-site as quickly as possible. Their contact numbers need to be prominently displayed.

Once the experts have been called, the management of a situation calls for the efficiency of key members of the team. Key team members might be health and safety representatives, managers and qualified first aiders. They should have their names and contact details prominently displayed at the setting and they should be readily accessible to manage a situation and also to give advice.

If there is not a well-thought-out plan, an emergency might cause chaos and people could lose their lives.

15.9 **Managing stress**

Common signs and indicators of stress

Signs and indicators of stress can often be mistaken for something else, such as simply being miserable (when that person is upset and irritable due to **stressors**).

Stress can be caused by trying to do too much

The way people behave when they experience stressful situations can vary.

- Physical signs include: headaches, stomach problems such IBS, nausea; sleep problems such as tiredness, lethargy, unable to sleep; skin complaints such as eczema, rashes and outbreaks of spots. Appetite may be poor or someone might overeat or drink too much alcohol.

- Cognitive signs are to do with thinking and reasoning. If you feel unable to cope, you may lose concentration and the ability to remember things. You may feel as if you cannot do things. Sometimes this is due to a loss of self-esteem and your thought patterns becoming negative. You may feel that other people's expectations are too high and you can feel like giving up. People who do not know you very well may interpret this kind of behaviour as inappropriate for the workplace and react badly. This makes feelings of low self-esteem even worse.

- Behavioural signs often result from those cognitive upsets and you might display uncharacteristic aggression, irritability or be withdrawn, timid, non-communicative or have difficulties relaxing.

- The worse-case scenario is if you feel it is not worth getting up in the morning, washing or looking after yourself properly so that your health suffers.

> 66 The occupations that reported the highest rates of work-related stress in the last three years were health and social service managers, teachers and social welfare associate professionals.
> 75 per cent of the new work-related conditions in 2010/11 were either musculoskeletal disorders or stress, depression and anxiety. 99

www.hse.gov.uk/stress

did you know?

According to MIND (the organisation for the promotion of better mental health) 'Every year over 5 million people have time off due to mental pressures at work'. www.mind.org.uk

Factors that tend to trigger stress

It is important to tackle the feelings of being unable to cope as soon as you experience them. Everyone is different in terms of how situations can affect them and make them feel. Your first challenge is to identify the stressors so that you can tackle them.

Stressors may be the result of work or home pressures, relationships, family or financial situations. A recent bereavement or break-up of a relationship can mean that you take longer than expected to get back to 'normal'.

think about

Make a list of all the things that make you feel 'under pressure' at work and at home. Share your list with a colleague or friend.

Strategies for managing stress

It is now considered a strength to admit you cannot cope. You are in fact analysing your feelings in order to enhance and improve your ability and performance in the workplace. Once you recognise the signs and indicators of stress, you can take steps to address how you feel.

What would you do?

Try this activity with a friend or colleague. Tick the boxes in the table below that apply to you and discuss the benefits that each strategy gives you.

Strategy	This is a must	Might try this	Not for me
Talking things through with someone I trust			
Arranging a supervision meeting with my line manager			
Having a massage or aromatherapy session			
Going for a long walk or a run			
Going to the gym			
Socialising with friends or going to watch a film			
Doing some voluntary work			
Creating or designing something			
Attending a course to improve my knowledge and skills			
Listening to music			

It may be that if you tried this activity every six months, your ticks would be in different places. For example, if you have just been turned down for a promotion you might consider further studying and discussions with your manager but if you have suffered a relationship breakdown you may opt for relaxation techniques or socialising with friends.

De-briefing times in the workplace are important, as are team meetings when stressful situations can be placed on the agenda for discussion along with group strategies for support, for example when understaffing occurs.

15.10 Procedures regarding handling medication

The main points of agreed procedures about handling medication

There are strict guidelines for storing, administering and disposing of medications in health and social care settings. The Handling of Medicines in Social Care (Royal Pharmaceutical Society, 2007) sets out eight key principles for medication handling. Principle 3 is that care staff should be competent to assist people with their medication.

Further legislation is set out in the 'Essential Standards of Quality and Safety', part of The Health and Social Care Act (2008). This competence is assessed in the workplace by the manager. Have a look at: www.rpharms.com/social-care-settings-pdfs/the-handling-of-medicines-in-social-care.pdf

In relation to storing medicines

Some drugs are addictive and might be dangerous in the wrong hands. These are referred to as controlled drugs and they must be stored separately in a locked cupboard within a locked cupboard that is rag bolted to the wall. A light will be displayed when the cupboard is opened that alerts others. These requirements are regulated by the Misuse of Drugs Act (Safe Custody) (1973).

Under the Essential Standards of Quality and Safety (Health and Social Care Act (2008)), Regulation 13 states:

'the registered person must protect individuals against the risks associated with the unsafe use and management of medicines, by making appropriate arrangements for the obtaining, recording, handling, using, safe keeping, dispensing, safe administration and disposal of medicines'.

The associated outcome is Outcome 9: 'People have their medicines when they need them and in a safe way. People are given information about their medicines'.

Other drugs are kept in a locked cupboard or in a locked trolley, which must not be left unattended.

Some medications such as eye drops or certain antibiotics must be stored in a lockable fridge (for the purpose of storing medications only).

Remember that care staff must be aware of their limitations when medicines need to be given.

Basic principles for administering medications

- Obtain the patient's (or resident's) consent to receive the medication.

- Wash your hands first and ensure the good hygiene of the individual receiving the medication. Using a non-touch technique is good practice.

- Identify the correct medication, dosage, strength, time and route for the correct patient (or resident).

- Use the MAR sheet (medicine administration record) to initial the medications given (once observed to be given).

- Monitor any effects of the medication and document this in the care plan as well as informing your manager of any adverse reactions.

Follow correct procedures for administering medication

Your basic training will involve assisting individuals to take their tablets, perhaps instilling eye drops or ear drops and applying topical creams and ointments. Specialised training may include:

- giving rectal preparations
- giving an insulin injection (subcutaneously)
- administering oxygen
- assisting with a nebuliser
- administering medication via a PEG.

These techniques cannot be performed without you first being assessed as competent by your manager. This will include knowledge of the medications that you administer to individuals in your care.

Under the Mental Capacity Act (2005), individuals have to be supported to understand their medications and treatments. Individuals must be given information about their medication in a way that they understand. The information is given to advocates or family members where the person's capacity to understand is limited.

As part of the Care Standards Act (2000), all individuals are encouraged to administer their own medicines independently. Carers and providers must risk assess an individual's capacity to self medicate and ensure that they understand how to store their medication, when to take it, how to take it , the possible side effects and benefits and when to alert staff of any concerns.

Carers administering medicines must be aware of the various routes for medications, the procedures for recording (using a MAR sheet), observing for any side effects and how to alert medical staff if there is a serious adverse reaction.

Controlled drugs are potentially addictive and dangerous and therefore are subject to strict regulatory guidance.

The amounts of controlled drugs to be administered are counted by two people and recorded in a special book along with the amount still remaining. A second person must witness the administering of the drug and countersign the amount given and the amount remaining. One of these people must be qualified to give out controlled drugs. This regulation leaves a clear **audit trail**.

find out!

Research some examples of controlled drugs and whether any are in use for the people you care for.

Audit trail A step-by-step record by which product (or financial) use can be traced, i.e. accounted for.

Key Terms

In some circumstances, you may need to contact the GP for instructions to change the dose of an existing medicine. Ensure that a colleague hears this instruction and that it does not involve a completely new medication. Note any changes in the care plan and check that the GP signs the MAR sheet as soon as possible.

In Practice

A colleague asks you to assist him with administering medications in the afternoon. The trolley is unlocked and taken into the community room where most of the residents are having afternoon tea. He suggests that you wash your hands and take some wipes on the trolley for the residents' hands. He advises that eye drops, pessaries, injections and inhalers will be administered in residents' own rooms. You also notice that he asks some residents if they are in pain and he tells you he needs to check the PRN on the MAR sheet.

Consequences of handling medication without specialised training

Simple instances of carelessness and not following agreed ways of working have led to mistakes.

What would you do?

You see some medicine pots in the kitchen with little tabs of paper in them indicating the residents' names. You realise that the morning medicines have been left out. What are the potential hazards of this practice and what would you do?

Complete the table below with the possible consequences for the individual, the carer and the residential home.

Incident	Consequences for the individual	Consequences for the carer	Consequences for the home
1 The medication was given to the wrong individual.			
2 The medication was double the intended dose.			
3 An adverse reaction was not reported.			
4 Some controlled drugs have gone missing.			

In each case there have been breaches of the law and, as you are accountable for your actions, you must report these types of errors.

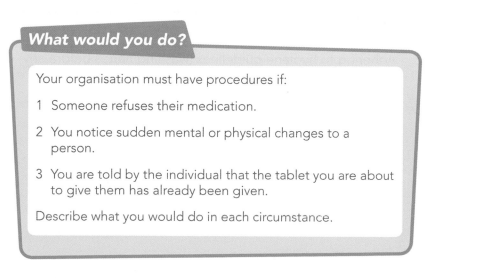

What would you do?

Your organisation must have procedures if:

1 Someone refuses their medication.

2 You notice sudden mental or physical changes to a person.

3 You are told by the individual that the tablet you are about to give them has already been given.

Describe what you would do in each circumstance.

15.11 Handling and storing food safely

The Food Safety Act (1990) states that you are in breach of the law if you sell or serve food that is unfit for eating and likely to make people ill.

The Food Hygiene (England) Regulations (2006) are mainly concerned with temperature control (adhering to strict guidelines on cooking to correct temperatures to kill off any pathogenic bacteria).

Regulation (EC) 852/2004 on the Hygiene of Foodstuffs sets out standards of acceptable hygiene on premises, including the hygiene of handlers, equipment used and training requirements.

If a complaint is investigated and it is discovered that people have been made ill by poor hygiene, poor temperature regulation and not adhering to standards, there are severe penalties such as prison and heavy fines.

Basically, there are two very important strands to food safety:

1. Adhering to temperature guidelines (cooking food to kill off any pathogenic bacteria). Re-heating is particularly hazardous as some residents may want to re-heat food until it is just warm, when in fact food should be re-heated to the same temperature as for cooking and never re-heated more than once.

2. Adhering to hygiene guidelines (washing hands before any duty, in between duties and after using the toilet).

Case study

In Practice

Adam, the senior care worker, is helping out in the kitchen as the home is holding a 'Cultural Foods' event. He washes his hands according to the correct procedure and puts on an apron and a hat.

He checks the list on the kitchen wall showing the names of the residents who have certain allergies to food and ensures that ingredients such as nuts, seeds, peanut oil and fish are not contained in the foods that they might eat.

He checks the dates on the chilled food and assists the chef wherever he can.

The chef asks him to check that the temperature of the fridge is about 5 degrees celsius before the sandwiches are made with cold fillings.

The chef uses a red chopping board for the raw meat and, when the meat is cooked, checks that the core temperature is 75 degrees celsius for at least two minutes. He explains to Adam that the cooked dish must be kept hot at 63 degrees celsius for no more than two hours. It is best that hot food is eaten straight away.

What would you do?

An individual wants to re-heat in the microwave some chicken pie that has been cooked and re-heated once already. What will you say to him?

Storing food

Incorrect storage can result from:

- placing raw foods next to cooked foods
- failing to store at the correct temperatures
- storing foods past their use by or best by date
- over-filling a fridge or freezer.

Maximise hygiene when handling food

The most important task when you are about to handle food is correct hand washing, described earlier in this unit (page 147). You should also pay attention to your nails, keeping them short and clean, and avoid nail varnish if you often handle food. Tie your hair back and wear a net or hat if that is the requirement of your organisation.

Inform your manager of any stomach upsets that you experience that involve diarrhoea and/or vomiting or respiratory infections. Be aware that you must not handle food or come to work for at least 48 hours until symptoms subside or are checked.

Your setting will use PPE (personal protective equipment), which may involve the wearing of hats, disposable gloves and aprons. It is still essential to wash hands before and after using gloves and aprons. It is also necessary to change a contaminated apron. Tasks performed in a kitchen must be carried out separately, for example preparing raw meat away from the preparation of cooked food (including sandwiches). If the same person performs both tasks, then scrupulous hand washing is essential together with the use of separate chopping boards. Ideally, prepare sandwiches first for chilled storage.

If you have a cut on your hand or fingers, you must cover it with a blue waterproof plaster. The waterproof element is a legal requirement.

There are some key considerations regarding the hygiene of the environment:

find out!

What are the ideal storing temperatures for fridges and freezers? How do you maintain them to make sure that they work well?

- Your equipment and utensils should be clean, including the probes that are used to check core temperatures of meat.

- A kitchen environment should legally contain two sinks, one for the washing of food and the other for hand washing.

- Tasks performed in a kitchen must be done separately: preparing raw meat to cook must be done away from the preparation of cooked food (including sandwiches).

- Clean all surfaces before starting food preparation tasks.

- Clean all sufaces and equipment with a sanitiser after food preparation and cooking.

- Use paper towels for cleaning.

- Make sure that cooked food is placed on clean plates and kept hot and covered.

- Make sure that cold food is maintained at a chilled temperature until the latest time possible and keep it covered.

Disposing of food

It is essential that you dispose of food so that no pests can find it. Food handlers should throw away food into bins with tightly fitting lids and this must be kept in a 'dirty area' waiting for collection.

Never leave deposits of food on plates in a dishwasher, especially overnight.

What could happen if an individual ate some leftover cooked chicken that had been left on a plate overnight in a warm room?

Potential consequences of not following food safety standards

Potential consequences for the individual

Gastroenteritis in older people may be complicated by severe dehydration. The individual may complain of thirst, have a dry tongue and sometimes appear confused. Re-hydration is the main treatment but medical advice must be sought.

The worst-case scenario of a food poisoning incident can be kidney damage and even death so it is very important to follow rigorous hygiene rules.

Potential consequences for the setting

If there was an outbreak of food poisoning in the setting, this would be investigated by the environmental health officer. If the outcome was serious, the local authority have the powers to close the home.

Generally, poor food hygiene is damaging to people's health especially those who are more vulnerable. This group includes older people, babies, young children and those with an **immuno-compromised** condition.

Immuno-compromised This means that people have weak immune systems and are not able to fight off micro-organisms as well as others.

Key Term

did you know?

'It's estimated there are more than nine million cases of gastroenteritis each year in England. For an increasing number of people, it is due to food poisoning, which is something that can be preventable.
Gastroenteritis describes symptoms affecting digestion, such as nausea, vomiting, diarrhoea and stomach pain. Food poisoning is the type of gastroenteritis caused by eating or drinking something contaminated with micro-organisms or germs, or by toxic substances produced by these germs. These illnesses are often accompanied by fever, muscle aches, shivering and feeling exhausted.'

www.bbc.co.uk/health

Quick Quiz

1   The legislation that sets out requirements for risk assessments is:
    a. The Health and Safety at Work Act (1974)
    b. Control of Substances Hazardous to Health
    c. The Management of Health and Safety Regulations (1999)
    d. Reporting of Injuries, Diseases and Dangerous Occurrences Regulations.

2   The second step of a risk assessment process is:
    a. identify the hazard
    b. review the risk assessment
    c. record the findings
    d. assess the risks.

3   In an emergency first aid situation, your main priority is to:
    a. stop the bleeding
    b. treat any fractures
    c. check the airway
    d. place immediately in the recovery position.

4   The most important task to do properly when considering hygiene is:
    a. wear gloves and aprons
    b. never touch anything that might be contaminated
    c. wash hands for 20 seconds using the correct procedure
    d. keep all surfaces clean and tidy.

5   Before moving and handling any individual, you must:
    a. seek consent and consult the handling care plan
    b. obtain a hoist
    c. do some stretches
    d. check with a physiotherapist.

6   Before using a new disinfectant, you must:
    a. open the windows in case of fumes
    b. obtain some clean uncontaminated cloths
    c. always dilute one part to ten
    d. read the manufacturer's instructions.

7   It is good practice to keep fire doors and corridors free from:
    a. clutter and combustible items
    b. clinical waste
    c. people
    d. trolleys.

8   Before handling and administering medication, it is essential that:
    a. you get to know the residents
    b. you know the pharmacist
    c. you have undergone training and been assessed as competent
    d. you wear an apron and and wash your hands.

9   Food poisoning is more likely to occur when:
    a. there has been poor hygiene
    b. food is brought in from outside
    c. food is piping hot
    d. food has been stored at the correct temperature.

10 Stressful situations are best dealt with by:
    a. drinking lots of alcohol
    b. having a quiet cry
    c. shouting at your partner or children
    d. talking over feelings with someone you trust.

Understand how
to handle information
in social care settings

This unit develops your knowledge and understanding of good practice in recording, sharing, storing and accessing information in social care settings. When you work in social care settings, you have to handle lots of different types of information relating to the clients you assist and support and the organisation you work for. Some of it will be spoken and some written. A lot of the information that you deal with will be confidential. You will also learn about supporting others in the way they handle information in social care settings.

On completion of this unit you should:

- understand requirements for handling information in social care settings

- understand good practice in handling information in social care settings

- understand how to support others to handle information

16.1 Understanding requirements for handling information

Staff must understand good practice in handling information

Legislation and codes of practice that relate to handling information

The main **legislation** affecting the recording, storage and sharing of information is outlined in the table on page 178. The law covers all kinds of information and **media**, not just written documents: it can include documents and emails on computers, information on CDs and memory sticks, as well as information that is shared verbally (spoken), for example on the telephone.

Legislation	What does it say?
Data Protection Act (1998)	Information should be: • used in ways that are fair, keep to the law and uphold a person's rights • recorded accurately, limited to just what is required and used only for the purpose you have stated • transferred or shared with others in ways that take proper precautions to keep it safe • stored in ways that are **secure** and kept no longer than is necessary
Human Rights Act (1998)	Even if a person is in care, or can no longer give their own consent for information about them to be shared, you must act in ways that make sure their privacy is respected.
Freedom of Information Act (2000)	Social care organisations must provide information about their policies and services. Clients (in most circumstances) must be allowed access to their own notes –usually by arrangement following a written request.
The Health and Social Care Act (2008)	This created the national Information **Governance** Board, which determines the policies and procedures relating to information handling that the employer has to follow.
Disability Discrimination Act (2005)	This requires employers and carers to take all reasonable steps to treat people with disabilities exactly the same as people without disabilities. It is just as important to respect disabled people's rights to do with information as anyone else's, even if they are unable to understand or realise that you are doing this. This Act is now part of the Equality Act (2010).
Various laws and case law relating to the protection of vulnerable adults	Adults who are identified as being vulnerable may be protected, or their abusers prosecuted, under various laws, depending on the offence committed against them. This could potentially include inadequate entries or fraudulent use of care records if this had a negative effect on the health or social care of an individual.

Legislation affecting information recording, storage and handling

Be sure to apply your understanding of legislation in an interview situation. You must not disclose any confidential information to prospective employers, or on your CV, so ensure that any examples that you give of your work are anonymous.

Codes of practice

Social care workers are required to follow or work within a number of codes of practice. These set out professional standards and guidelines for social care practice. Your employer or professional organisation (e.g., the General Social Care Council – GSCC) will produce codes of practice about information handling that you should know about and understand.

Ask your manager about the arrangements where you work for giving a client access to their personal files.

Reflecting the law in your working practice

The ways in which you handle information at work – the things you do, say and write – must follow the law and codes of practice. The individuals you provide care for have the right to have their information recorded correctly, stored safely and only shared with those people who need to know about it. To achieve high standards of practice in handling information, you should:

- be able to justify the purpose of every item of information requested

- only share an individual's personal information with others if absolutely necessary

- use the minimum amount of personal information necessary to do a particular task

- access personal information on a strict need-to-know basis only

- be aware of your responsibilities when accessing personal information

- understand and comply with the law.

Know when to share confidential information

16.2 **Understand good practice in handling information in social care settings**

Social care workers deal with a range of different types of information on a daily basis. Look back at the table on page 178 to remind yourself of the main types of information you are likely to come across. A social care worker needs to be able to receive information – both written and spoken – record it, store it, pass it on and sometimes dispose of it. Each stage of this process must be carried out correctly.

Recording and storing information correctly

At work you will need to identify information that is relevant to the care and needs of clients before recording it accurately and storing it safely in:

 paper-based files

 computer-based files

a smart phone or electronic notebook

portable devices, such as a memory stick/pen.

You must ensure that it is secure. Once personal information, such as a phone message, is no longer needed it must also be disposed of appropriately. If information about people is not handled correctly, individuals who should not see it might see it. Alternatively, it may be damaged, stolen or lost, any of which may have serious consequences. Remind yourself about the main ways to deal with a variety of different types of information by looking back at the table on page 167 of level two.

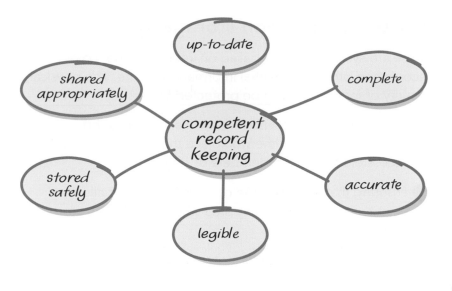

Competent record keeping is essential

Ask a senior colleague how long personal records about clients must be retained in your work setting and find out the measures taken to make sure that these are completed correctly, kept securely and later disposed of safely.

Using manual and electronic information storage systems

There may be a manual or an electronic (computer-based) information storage system within your workplace, or a mixture of the two. It is important to understand how each of these systems provides information security so that you can use them appropriately.

You must know how to use the computer securely

Legible Refers to writing that is easy to read, especially handwriting.

Key Terms

Have you ever read what a doctor or other care worker has written in care records about you or a relative? Was it helpful to do this?

How do you keep personal information and important documents secure at home?

Manual information storage systems

These are systems that are based on keeping paper-based records and other confidential information secure. The physical security of information can be protected by:

- keeping confidential information in a locked cupboard or cabinet in an area of the workplace that is discreet and only accessible to specific members of staff

- ensuring that visitors to the care setting are not allowed unsupervised access to any area where records are stored or may be accessible

- never leaving care records, notes or reports open in public areas of the care setting and ensuring that staff cannot be overheard when making or receiving telephone calls about clients or care-related issues.

As well as ensuring that records are stored securely, you must also ensure that information relating to individuals is recorded correctly and appropriately. For example:

- Each individual's name should be clearly marked on their records so that you are clear about whose record or notes you are completing.

- Your handwriting must be **legible**, avoiding abbreviations and jargon (for example, 'ENT' for Ear, Nose and Throat Department) so that others don't misunderstand what you have written.

- You should only include information that is relevant and objective so that your co-workers can rely on information being appropriate, in the right place and available to those who might need to know it, as well as protected from those who don't.

- Write up notes as soon as possible after you obtain information – you may not remember all the details later on. This could be very important if the notes are ever used in court.

Electronic information storage systems

Information relating to social care clients is now often created and stored on computer-based devices such as computers, mobile phones and memory sticks. **Encrypting files** and emails protects the security of confidential computer-based information. This makes it impossible to access or read them without the use of approved passwords. Guidelines for using electronic information systems include:

- Always protect and never share your computer password.

- Ensure that you close files and log-off properly when you have finished reading or adding information to a client's computer-based files.

- Change your password(s) regularly and never write them down.

- Work on one record at a time, saving your work regularly to ensure that you don't enter information in the wrong record or lose what you have written if you are distracted or called away.

- Only use an individual's initials and the minimum personal information in a 'public' communication or if you are replying to an email sent by someone from outside of your care organisation.

- Follow good record-keeping practice in making sure that what you write is spelt correctly, concise, avoids abbreviations, is factual and is written as soon as possible after the event.

- Find out whether there are specific rules in your workplace about deleting files or parts of client's files that you or others have created. If in doubt, don't delete anything.

- Laptop computers and memory sticks should only be used to store client-related information when you have your employer's permission to do so. Both are easily lost, may be stolen and are insecure. If they are used in your work setting, laptop computers and memory sticks should always be kept in a securely locked drawer, cupboard or cabinet.

Encrypted files Electronic files protected by a code that can only be accessed by means of a password.

Key Term

Tip

REED SOCIAL CARE

Ensure that you maintain accurate records of your work and training history. Store training and qualification certificates securely, as you may be asked to produce them by a recruitment agency or prospective employer as proof of any training you have undertaken.

How are your own medical or care records recorded? Are they kept on computer or paper-based files? Are all of your personal and contact details up-to-date?

Keeping records up-to-date

Tasks such as writing in someone's care file, recording medication that you have given to an individual and making notes about conversations should be done as soon as possible after you have carried them out so you do not forget any essential information. Some records, such as medication charts, require the time to be recorded as well as signing and dating. Make sure that any information from outside the workplace, such as professional reports, are filed in accordance with your organisation's record-keeping system, making them easy to find. Periodically check with clients (or their relatives) if contact information (address, email, telephone numbers) is up-to-date.

Case study

In Practice

Sajid has been asked to encourage a new, physically disabled individual who has a urinary tract infection to drink plenty of fluids. Sajid has a fluid intake chart to complete. He also has a pottery group to run, as well as a number of reports to write by the end of the day. One individual complains of feeling lightheaded during the pottery group but feels better when she goes into the garden for fresh air, then another cuts her finger on a pottery tool.

1. What do you recommend Sajid does to make sure that he remembers all the information correctly?

2. What different types of records will Sajid need to complete?

3. Identify two things Sajid needs to do to record and store information correctly.

Your questions answered

> **What should I do about incomplete records?**
>
> Make sure that you know the rules in your workplace about when and how often you need to record something in a client's file. If a record is incomplete, *never* make up information to fill the gap. Instead, inform a senior member of staff immediately. You may then be asked to contact an outside practitioner, or talk with your co-workers (colleagues) who were present at the time in question in order to complete the record accurately.

Ensuring that records are accurate

As well as being up-to-date and complete, the details of individual entries in someone's records must also be correct, especially who said or did what. Only record what you have done yourself, and sign only for yourself. If you are asked by a senior staff member to record something on their behalf, make this clear in what you write. If a family member asks you to put something in a client's file, record their name and make it clear that you are quoting information supplied by someone other than yourself. Finally, be extra careful when recording numbers and quantities – particularly when it comes to administering prescribed drugs or dealing with an individual's money.

Sharing information appropriately

Information must only be given to those who really need to know it. It is equally important to make sure that information is passed on when it is needed. This includes information you have gained from clients about their needs or preferences, especially if these have changed. Colleagues or visiting practitioners may need brief information about a client, especially if the person has communication difficulties. If you are worried about any change in an individual, you should report it privately, away from the client and others. In the same way, any new information about a person – provided, for example, by a district nurse – should be recorded and shared with a senior member of staff. Always share and record information in an objective way that avoids criticising, judging or demeaning the individual.

Case study

In Practice

Kay works in a supported living bungalow with two young women who have complex physical and learning disabilities. The residents have argued about where they should go on holiday this year. This has led to several incidents where the two women shout at each other and end up crying. Neither has hit or physically hurt the other but both are still very upset. Kay was on duty when the last episode of crying and shouting occurred. She has now been asked by her manager to complete an incident form explaining what has been happening. Yesterday, Kay talked to her colleague Dan about what she would write and who she thought was to blame while they took the women out for a walk in the local park.

1. Should Kay and her colleague have had this discussion within earshot of the clients?

2. What information do you think is relevant to include on the incident form?

Confidential information and knowing how to manage it securely

Social care workers need to know personal information about their clients in order to provide appropriate support and assistance, for example details about their family and their life. You will probably need to share information like this with other practitioners, such as social workers.

Some of this information will be confidential and you must know how to deal with this in a professional way. Remember, you must not share information outside the workplace about the people you care for, even if you do not use their name. It is never alright to gossip. You must also make sure that confidential information is not overheard or seen by the wrong people.

Confidentiality

Confidentiality does not mean keeping things secret. It means making sure that only people who need to know, or have a right to know **confidential information** have access to it. Social care organisations will have a written confidentiality policy that sets out procedures about the correct ways to handle confidential information. Make sure that you read this, understand it and know how it applies to your everyday working.

Ask to see the confidentiality policy at your place of work. Take time to read it carefully, making notes about those aspects that directly affect your working practice. Ask a senior colleague or your supervisor about anything you don't understand.

How do you know whether information is confidential?

The different types of information you will be expected to handle that are confidential may concern:

- physical and mental health status and history
- personal details to do with identity, such as religion and sexual orientation
- physical measurements such as weight and height
- test and investigation results, such as blood and urine tests and x-rays

> ### What would you do?
>
> On the bus home, you overhear a couple of colleagues discussing intimate and confidential information about an individual you all work with. How would you feel about this? What could you say to stop your colleagues speaking in this way?

> **Confidential information**
> Information that may only be shared with those who have a good reason and the authority or permission to know it.
>
> ### Key Term

family information regarding relationships and personal history

financial and legal matters.

When information is confidential individuals might say things like, 'to be shared on a "need to know" basis only.' If you are unsure about who 'needs to know', ask a senior member of staff. If there is no one available, assume that information is confidential and cannot be shared until you have an opportunity to check.

What would you do?

Cheryl has recently completed her induction training as a community support worker. Henry is one of the first clients she works with. Henry has early-stage dementia but is also suffering from lung cancer. When Cheryl was leaving Henry's house after a recent visit, a neighbour started talking to her about 'poor Henry'. Cheryl chatted back while walking down the street, saying that it's really sad that Henry has terminal cancer as well as the problems caused by dementia. She ends the conversation by saying that 'he'll need full time care soon, I'd say. Probably have to move to a home'.

What information is acceptable and unacceptable for Cheryl to share with the neighbour?

What would you say to the neighbour if they asked about Henry's condition and you were his support worker?

How do you think you would feel if a doctor or care worker disclosed personal or medical details about you without your permission?

When must confidentiality be broken?

Social care workers must sometimes go against the normal rules about confidentiality. It is acceptable, and may be a legal requirement, to disclose confidential information if doing so will protect clients or other people from harm. A social care worker may, depending on the circumstances, need to disclose confidential information to the police, or a doctor, if an individual's physical safety or health is 'at risk'. It is acceptable to breach confidentiality when:

a person is at risk of harm, such as showing suicidal behaviour

a person has committed, or is about to commit, a crime

the health or safety of others is at risk

abuse of a child or adult is disclosed or suspected

a court orders certain information to be disclosed.

16.3 Understand how to support others to handle information

Social care workers tend to work in teams with co-workers who may also be social care staff or with people from other care backgrounds as part of multi-disciplinary and even multi-agency teams. You may take on responsibility for supporting less experienced co-workers or people who are new to your team. As part of this role, you may be asked to:

- ensure that others understand the need for secure handling of information

- ensure that others access relevant compulsory training (for example information governance)

- support others to put into practice the guidance and procedures from information governance

- ensure that others understand the importance of secure record keeping

- support and enable others to contribute to manual and electronic records (for example reporting accurate and sufficient information to the appropriate people, sharing relevant information about any changes in an individual's personal details, condition or care needs

- ensure that others are familiar with procedures for reporting incidents relating to any breach of information security such as missing, lost, damaged or stolen information or records.

Ensure that your colleagues understand the need to keep information secure

The organisation or agency employing you should have written policies and procedures about information handling and security. You should be able to support co-workers and others (such as students) so that they:

- know where they can find policies and procedures relating to information handling and governance

- understand what the policies and procedures say about information handling practices in the workplace

- can apply the policies and procedures about handling to their particular work role.

The type and level of support that your co-workers need to handle information appropriately will depend on their previous experience, level of ability and current work role. Bearing this in mind, you can support them by:

- identifying the parts of the policies and procedures that are most relevant for them

- providing practical examples of how to put the policies and procedures into practice. This could involve showing a person what to do in different circumstances.

If colleagues are new or inexperienced, start by showing them the various types and sections of care records before they are asked to make any entries. They should be shown examples in the records of entries that are up-to-date, complete, accurate and legible. They should also be shown examples of where information has been stored safely and shared appropriately.

You may need to find ways of explaining the main reasons for secure handling of information and why confidentiality is an important issue for all social care workers. It is best to encourage new staff to always ask questions about information handling and security issues if they are unsure or become concerned about them. You should also encourage and support other staff to make use of induction and other regular training opportunities relating to information handling issues. This will help them to understand in more detail the policies and procedures (and the reasons behind them) relating to information governance.

What would you do?

What did you find difficult or confusing when you were first asked to start contributing to care records? How might you use this experience to show or explain to newer staff more clearly how to contribute to people's records?

Case study

In Practice

Andy has worked in a care home for frail older people for two months. He is supervised by a senior care worker, and they share a line manager. Andy was given a computer password and shown where the resident's paper-based records are kept during his induction training. He knows how to send emails to co-workers and his manager and how to complete the computer-based documents used in the care home.

1. If you were in Andy's position, what questions would you ask about information handling relating to your work role?

2. Where would you suggest Andy looks for help if he has problems with information handling issues?

Handling confidential information – a UK Local Authority

When handling confidential information, our staff need to follow the same good practices day in, day out, without losing concentration. It can be difficult to maintain the same high standards at all time, but the privacy and right to confidentiality of our clients needs to be respected, and anybody who works here needs to show an appreciation of that.

@work

When you are in a position of responsibility, your own information handling practices should provide a model for others to follow. Remember that any breach of confidentiality, inappropriate use of care records, or any abuse of secure computer systems, may lead to disciplinary measures being taken against yourself or others. This could ultimately lead to your prosecution and dismissal if the breach is severe. You should ensure that you never breach information security procedures and should always report any possible or actual breaches of security or confidentiality that occur.

Quick Quiz

1 Which of the following laws affects the recording, storage and handling of information in social care settings?
   a. The Community Care Act (1990)
   b. The Mental Health Act (1983)
   c. The Data Protection Act (1998)
   d. The Computer Misuse Act (2002)

2 Which of the following legal obligations is imposed on social care organisations by the Freedom of Information Act (2000)?
   a. Ensuring that an individual's daily activity and progress is documented.
   b. Allowing individuals access to information held about them following a written request.
   c. Keeping records relating to clients for a minimum of five years after discharge.
   d. Allowing clients' next of kin access to information help about them following a written request.

3 A manual information storage system is used to keep which of the following types of information secure?
   a. Computer files
   b. Phone messages
   c. Paper-based records
   d. All of the above

4 Which of the following are indicators of competent record-keeping in social care settings?
   a. Up-to-date and complete entries
   b. Legible and jargon-free handwriting
   c. Objective and accurate reporting of daily events
   d. All of the above

5 Shah is a new support worker in a residential care home. He has forgotten his computer password. Should Darren, Shah's supervisor, share his own password to enable Shah to make an entry in a resident's records?
   a. Yes, but warn him not to disclose it.
   b. No, ask Shah to request a new password.
   c. Yes, but stay with Shah until he logs off the computer.
   d. No, Darren should ask Shah to give him the information and make the entry in the resident's record himself.

6 Confidentiality in relation to social care record keeping involves:
   a. keeping information about a client's health or personal circumstances secret
   b. restricting access to personal and sensitive information about clients to people who need to know or have a right to know
   c. being confident in the way that you write in client's records
   d. never disclosing to others information that a client gives to you 'in confidence'.

7 Stephen is a middle-aged man who has recently become homeless after spending all of his money to fund his addiction to cocaine. Which of the following items of information about Stephen should be treated as confidential?
   a. His drug addiction
   b. The breakdown of his marriage
   c. His hostel address
   d. All of the above

Quick Quiz (continued)

8   Confidential information relating to a social care client can be disclosed if:

   a. most members of the care team are aware of it anyway

   b. the health or safety of the client or others is at risk

   c. the information has already been discussed in a staff meeting

   d. you insist you only reveal it to your friend or partner 'in confidence'.

9   Kelly has just started at Octagon Housing Trust as a support worker. How can Hannah, her supervisor, support Kelly in developing her information-handling skills?

   a. Teach Kelly the short cuts and abbreviations that experienced support workers use when completing clients' records.

   b. Book Kelly a place on the next course about information-handling issues.

   c. Show Kelly where the policies and procedures about information handling are and explain the key parts to her.

   d. Tell Kelly not to worry about this for a while as she won't need to write in anybody's records until after she has completed her induction.

10 A breach of confidentiality or other information-handling procedures at work could, in the worst case, lead to a social care worker being:

   a. disciplined and suspended

   b. given a verbal warning

   c. given a final written warning

   d. prosecuted and dismissed.

Ready for work?

Throughout this course you have been furnished with the tools to successfully apply for positions within the adult social care sector.

What follows is a checklist of things you should have done during the course to ensure that you are well placed to successfully apply and interview for the positions which interest you.

Checklist

☑ **CV** – produce a concise, well presented CV that complies with data confidentiality (see reed.co.uk for advice).

☑ **Work experience** – try to obtain some voluntary work experience to strengthen your application. Speak to local organisations to see if you can work with them.

☑ **Research** – make a list of local companies that you feel you would like to work for and find out what they do. Researching these companies at this stage will make applying to work for them later much easier. It will also help a recruitment agency find a suitable position for you if you have a good understanding of the types of organisation you would like to work for.

☑ **Extra activities** – think about extra activities that you have done or could do to strengthen your CV by demonstrating leadership skills, inspiration and improvement.

☑ **Weaknesses** – think about any areas in your skills and experience that you feel could be improved. These are essential for interview, and you should also think about ways to improve them.

☑ **Interview practice** – practise interview questions with your friends or family, to improve your confidence when you attend the real thing. Look online at reed.co.uk for tips on interview questions, and example questions that you might be asked.

☑ **Personal Development Plan (PDP)** – create a PDP, detailing your training experience and courses that you would like to take in the future. This will help you to have a clear idea about where you would like your career to go. This kind of information can also be helpful to any recruitment agency that you may choose to visit.

☑ **References** – these are essential if you want to work in the social care sector. As you come to the end of any voluntary work, make sure you obtain the details of somebody you can ask for a reference when applying for future jobs. Also, keep track of people from your time in education – if you do not have much professional experience, educational references will be important. You should keep a list of these references in your work pack – they will be asked for by both recruitment agencies and any prospective employers that you apply to work for.

Applying for jobs

Now that you have successfully created your CV using advice from reed.co.uk, you are ready to start applying for jobs. The following checklist gives a number of steps that you should take to ensure that you have the best chance of finding the job you want.

Checklist

☑ **Set up email alerts** – use reed.co.uk to set up an email alert which will come through to you when new jobs are posted in the social care sector. This will enable you to apply quickly when new jobs are posted, as well as keeping you aware of opportunities in the market.

☑ **Apply for jobs online** – using reed.co.uk, search for positions in the social care sector that are near where you live. If you find something that interests you, then apply! Write a brief covering letter to accompany your CV – make sure that it makes specific reference to the position that you are applying for, but don't make it too long.

☑ **Register with your local Reed Social Care branch** – phone or visit them to make an appointment to do this. When meeting a consultant, ensure that you take along all the documentation that you have been asked to bring – you won't be able to register without it. Registering with a Reed consultant means that you increase your chances of finding the right job for you. You should be honest about your skills and experience, as that will aid the consultant in matching you to jobs that would interest and benefit you. Reed Social Care has a variety of temporary and permanent positions available throughout the UK.

Glossary

Accountable Answerable to someone or responsible for some action.

Adult at risk Anyone aged 18 years and over who might not be able to protect themselves because they are ill, disabled or older.

Advocacy Speaking up on behalf of an individual, to express their views and protect their rights.

Anaphylactic shock A severe allergic reaction that causes breathing difficulties, swelling and possibly unconsciousness.

Argyle's communication cycle Ideas occur, message coded, message sent, message received, message decoded, message understood.

Aseptic technique A non-touch method of cleaning and dressing a wound, maintaining a sterile field – the working area that is completely free of possible harmful micro-organisms (germs) and is not contaminated (touched) by anything that is not sterile.

Attachment relationship A relationship that is based on strong emotional bonds.

Audit trail Step-by-step record by which product (or financial) use can be traced, i.e. accounted for.

Autonomy Independent and free to act.

Bio-hazards Anything that is biologically hazardous to people or the environment.

Caldicott Guardian A Caldicott Guardian is a senior person responsible for protecting the confidentiality of service-user and patient information; and enabling appropriate information-sharing.

Capacity The mental or physical ability to do something.

Cardiac arrest This means the heart has stopped beating.

Code of practice A set of guidelines and expectations that must be followed.

Coerce Force someone to do something against their will.

Collude Co-operate with somebody in order to do something illegal or to keep it secret.

Commission Deliberately doing something while knowing the consequences.

Concept An abstract idea – often thought about through analysis of situations.

Confidential Information is only shared with those who have a good reason and the authority or permission to know it.

Confidential information Information that may only be shared with those who have a good reason and the authority or permission to know it.

Confidentiality This means keeping information private when it does not need to be shared, or must not be shared.

Conflict This can be useful in understanding the other person's worries and needs because it arises from deeply held beliefs.

Consent Giving informed agreement to or permission for something to happen, such as an action or decision. Establishing consent varies according to individual's assessed capacity to give consent.

Constructive feedback Feedback that is intended to build on previous knowledge and used to improve performance and competence. It can be misinterpreted as criticism.

Continuous personal development (CPD)
Evidence that an individual or team is continually keeping up to date, improving themselves and the organisation in which they work.

CPR CPR means Cardio-Pulmonary Resuscitation (Cardio refers to the heart, pulmonary refers to the lungs and resuscitation is to recover the breathing and circulatory cycle).

Delegation Giving responsibility to someone to fulfill a certain task or aspect of work.

Deliberate discrimination Discrimination against a person or a group of people as a direct result of a purposeful action or omission.

Diabetes Diabetes is a condition which, because of the body's failure to produce insulin (a hormone that controls sugar levels in the blood), results in the person feeling unwell. This may progress to unconsciousness unless treated.

Dignity Closely related to human rights; dignity is about the idea of respect and status and is at the core of person-centred value.

Disability A physical and mental impairment which has a long term, substantial and adverse impact on normal day to day activities.

Diversity Differences in culture, ability, ethnicity, gender, age, beliefs, sexual orientation and social class.

Emotional intelligence Includes being self-aware; controlling impulsive reactions; being motivated and socially acute.

Empower To give power or authority to a person or group and to enable or permit them to do something.

Empowerment Gaining more control over your life by having opportunities to develop greater self-confidence and self-esteem.

Encrypted files Electronic files protected by a code that can only be accessed by means of a password.

Equality Promoting equal rights and opportunities for everyone.

Ergonomics Fitting a task to the individual, their capabilities, strength, stability and mental capacity. It can involve the use of aids.

Ethos Believing in a particular pathway or style. An example is a home that gives a definite impression of personalised individual care or a school whose ethos is to achieve high standards is top of the league table.

Feedback Refers to comments on our performance and is best made in a positive reflective way, for example-'How do you think you did?' followed by some good comments and then how you could improve.

Five senses The senses used for communication are hearing, sight and touch. The other two are smell and taste.

Foreseeable To be aware of beforehand, or to be able to accurately anticipate something happening.

Formal relationship A relationship that is based on agreed, formal rules between employers and employees and with colleagues in a workplace.

Governance Procedures and checks to ensure that the correct rules are followed.

Holistic Describes the person as a whole; their physical, psychological, social and spirtiual characteristics and needs.

Homophobia An irrational dislike, hatred or fear of individuals who are lesbian, gay, bisexual or transgendered.

Human rights An international set of rules stating what everyone needs to live and grow.

Hypoglycaemic condition When a person feels unwell due to the lack of sugar in the circulation. People with diabetes cannot convert sugar into glucose or energy for the body and this has to be given quickly or they will collapse.

Immuno-compromised This means that people have weak immune systems and therefore not able to fight off micro-organisms as well as others.

Inadvertent discrimination A situation of unequal outcomes or disadvantage for individuals or groups resulting from an action or omission that is not in itself discrimination.

Inclusive practice Working in a way that aims to include an individual or group in a positive manner by valuing their difference rather than seeing it as an issue to overcome.

Invasive procedures Inserting pessaries or suppositories.

Legible Refers to writing that is easy to read, especially handwriting.

Legislation Laws, in this case governing the use of information.

Media Different ways of recording or conveying information, for example print or video.

Mediation Negotiation to resolve issues by neutral individual (service).

Medical model of disability The medical model looks at what is 'wrong' with the person and what needs to be 'fixed' or treated, in contrast to the social model.

Moral Describes behaving in a way that is good and appropriate.

Multi-agency working An arrangement where workers from different agencies or organisations work together.

Multi-disciplinary working This is where different care professionals work together in the same team.

Negotiation This involves finding a solution that is acceptable to both parties, leaving everyone feeling that they have achieved a positive outcome.

Non-verbal communication skills Includes using eye contact; affirmative actions such as nodding; allowing silence and relaxing your body.

Norm Accepted, normal behaviour.

Omission Where something is either deliberately or accidentally not done.

Pathogenic bacteria These are harmful bacteria that can make you ill.

PEG feeding A specialised technique that enables medicines to be administered straight into the stomach (percutaneous endoscopic gastrostomy).

Person-centred care planning
Person-centred thinking skills – considering the person as a whole, and as part of their own network; Total communication – including meeting the person's communication needs and active listening; Essential lifestyle planning – how their lifestyle contributes to their well-being; Person-centred reviews – evaluating the person's care while paying attention to other changes going on around them.

Plain English Communication styles that are clear, brief and to the point and avoid technical language, particularly in relation to official communication.

PPE Personal and protective equipment consists of aprons, disposable gloves, hats and a uniform. They are barriers between the carer and the person (or food) intended to be protected from infection.

Protocol Set of standardised procedures.

Qualification and Credit Framework (QCF) A bank of educational courses that carry points (credits) for learning. These credits are held centrally so that learners can build on them by completing a range of short courses (at varying levels of learning) that are relevant to them. A qualification will have rules of combination to say which units of learning make up the qualification as a whole.

Regulation of Controlled Drugs Controlled drugs (CDs) are strictly regulated because they are potentially addictive and open to abuse.

Religion and belief Any religious belief or similar philosophical belief described by these three criteria collective worship, a clear belief system, a profound belief affecting a way of life or view of the world.

Response Responses to a message may be verbal – including words used, tone, pitch or even silence; non-verbal – including body language, facial expressions, eye contact, gestures and touch.

Retribution Something done to injure, punish or 'get back' at someone.

Risk assessments Steps taken to ensure that any potential hazards are assessed and the chances of the hazard occurring is reduced by taking preventive steps.

Risk enablement Getting the balance right between risk taking and being risk averse while paying attention to the issues of safeguarding and the professional's duty of care.

Risk taking Enabling and supporting the person to make informed choices and decisions by understanding and taking responsibility for their actions and the consequences.

Safeguarding Ensuring the individual is safe from abuse and neglect, and helping people to make choices independently.

Secure Information that is not just physically safe (e.g. in a locked cabinet), but also protected from people who do not need to know about it.

Sexism Conduct or words or practices which disadvantage or advantage people because of their gender, marital status or caring responsibilities. It includes both gender and sexual harassment.

Sexual harassment Unwanted conduct of a sexual nature or other conduct based on sex affecting the dignity of men and women.

Sexual orientation Attraction to the opposite sex, the same sex, both sexes or neither sex.

Socialisation The way in which a person learns about the world around them, and the values and expectations of the society they live in.

Social model of disability The social model of disability relates closely to inclusive practice. It describes disability as being caused by the way society is organised, rather than by the individual's difference. When physical barriers and attitudes that restrict life choices are removed, disabled people can function in society in an equal way.

Standard procedures Approved ways of working to be followed routinely.

Standing aid Equipment used to assist a person to stand, the person must able to bear some of their weight and be able to co-operate.

Stressors Anything that can cause or trigger feelings of being unable to cope or manage day-to-day activities or a particular lifestyle choice.

Subcutaneous injections Injections where a short needle is inserted just under the skin with a small needle. You will require special training to administer them.

Unsafe practice An approach or standard of care that puts individuals at risk.

Verbal communication skills Includes checking, clarifying, encouraging, reflecting, affirming and summarising.

Vulnerable More likely to suffer risk and harm.

Vulnerable groups These include older people, babies and children, pregnant women and people with low resistance to infections, sometimes referred to as 'immuno-compromised'.

Well-being Factors such as biological, health, spiritual, emotional, cultural, religious, social satisfaction come together to create a person's well being.

Whistle-blowing Raising or communicating a disclosure in the public interest.

Index